Life in the Middle

Life in the Middle

C. SCOTT FOWLER

Issachar Imprints | Smithtown, New York

Life in the Middle and
Life in the Middle **Discovery Guide**

Contact Issachar Imprints at publish-
er@issacharimprints.com

ISBN: 978-0-578-17284-2

First Printing, December 2015

For Penny, Seth, Katie, and Grayson

CONTENTS

CONTENTS

Acknowledgments

I have preached and taught the principles in this book for over twenty years and have many times thought to write them down in book form. That day has finally come. I want to acknowledge those who, over the years, in places like Texas and Tennessee, Minnesota and Oklahoma, and, in the last nine years, here in New York, have put up with me, encouraged me, forgiven me, rejected me, challenged me, dialogued with me, agreed with me, disagreed with me, ignored me, taught me, and allowed me to teach them. Thank you. You have shaped me and, thus, the material in this book.

I want to thank Louis Block, Linda Carroll, Alex Coutrier, Karyn Craft, Judy Ligon, Jimmy Mangogna, Deanne Schram, and Debbie Spreckels who were willing to read the manuscript. The book is better because of their feedback.

Many thanks to *my* pastor, Gary Zarlengo, who allows me to minister freely in the area of my giftings.

Of course, I want to thank my wife Penny and my three children Seth, Katie, and Grayson who have loved me truer than anyone for the last twenty-seven years.

Finally, to the reader: thank you for giving this book a shot. I hope it will bless you and encourage you as you endeavor to live your life faithfully in the middle, between promise and fulfillment.

Introduction

We live our lives in the middle—between the "now" and the "not yet." For now, we have tasted of the Lord and seen that He is good, but we have not yet seen and experienced all He has planned for us. God is with us in the middle, leading us forward. But exactly in *what way* is God with us? How does He lead us forward? Scripture has much to say about how God works with us, shapes us, and moves us.

In the Bible, there are some amazing, inspiring accounts of God's involvement in the lives of His people. While these stories do not always yield a hard and fast formula by which we can define God's ways, they do reveal some observable elements which I call *God's process.*

Sometimes, we suffer the *death of the vision.* That is, we experience the failure of our own plans to come to fruition. But in God's process, we learn that the loss of *our* vision makes room for the birth of *His*. Our own plans must give way or die before we are able to see God's plans come to fruition. God's process is the way God chooses to move us from where we are to where He wants us to be.

One of the greatest realities about God is that He chooses to do what He does *in participation with us*. That is, He chooses to draw us into a cooperative relationship with Himself that allows us to participate in what He is doing in our lives and in the world. In His process, as God moves us from *divine dissatisfaction* through *divine imagination* to victory and rejoicing, He teaches us how to wait on Him—one of the chief ways we participate with God.

In *Part 1* of this book, we will take a glimpse at what it means to live life "in the middle." We will observe the process whereby God moves us from *our* vision to the fulfillment of *His* vision for our lives.

In *Part 2*, we will see how these principles played out in two particular lives that were lived victoriously in the middle—the lives of Hannah and Habakkuk.

In *Part 3*, we will take a fresh look at what it *really* means to wait on the Lord—a vital part of life in the middle! Far from being a passive stalling of progress, waiting on the Lord is a strong, active approach to the Christian life that brings God's power to bear in every situation.

As part of our discussion on waiting on the Lord, we will see what *worldview* has to do with it. We will take a brief look at the *anatomy of disillusionment*, and pose three simple yet extremely important questions. Finally, we will discover the power of knowing God's purpose, the importance of locating our lives in the larger picture of the spiritual realm, understanding the significance of God's timing, tapping into the power of the simple yet profound principle of *reckoning*, and embracing God as our portion.

Before moving forward . . .

My hope is that this book will inspire you, spark your imagination, and breathe meaning into the life *you* are living in the middle. At the end of every chapter, before moving forward to the next, we will consider together some things that will help us apply the truths of each chapter to our own situations.

So, before we go deeper into this concept of "middle living," would you take a moment to invite God into whatever you are walking through? Perhaps this book has not found you at your best—middle living can be discouraging at times. But be assured: if you belong to Him, He is with you in the middle!

Part 1

Life in the Middle

In these first chapters you will need your imagination. Not because what you will read is fictional. On the contrary, the pictures painted here are as real as they come. The problem is us! We rarely take the time to allow the realities of Scripture to "sink-in."

As you move forward, take the time to look up the Bible passages mentioned. Allow yourself to consider how the various characters mentioned may have felt. As you learn about God's process, consider where *you* are in that process. Ask yourself in what ways God has invited *you* to participate with Him in what He is doing in the world today.

1

Between Promise and Fulfillment

In the Book of Habakkuk, God revealed to the prophet that a terrible purging time was about to descend upon Judah because of its sins. God would use Babylon to destroy Jerusalem and wreak such havoc that Jeremiah in the Book of Lamentations would write,

> Look, O LORD, and consider: Whom have you ever treated like this? Should women eat their offspring, the children they have cared for? Should priest and prophet be killed in the sanctuary of the Lord (Lamentations 2:20)?

As Habakkuk came to grips with this realization, coupled with the God-given vision of a day when, "the earth will be filled with the knowledge of the glory of the LORD, as the waters cover the sea (Habakkuk 2:14)," he prayed to God saying,

> O LORD, I have heard thy speech, and was afraid: O LORD, revive thy work in the midst of the years, In the midst of the years make known; In wrath remember mercy (Habakkuk 3:2, KJV).

Habakkuk was living life in the middle; between the "now" and the "not yet"; between promise and fulfillment (please see APPENDIX).

What is life in the middle?

Life in the middle is living for God by faith in the midst of what seem to be impossibilities. It is not resignation to compromise and defeat but rather patient expectancy as we wait for the fulfillment of all that God has promised. It is life lived *between* promise and fulfillment. This is a key point. Unless one has heard and received the promise, he or she has no reason to hope for its fulfillment!

The Bible is chock full of examples of people, just like you and me, who lived godly lives in the tension that exists between promise and fulfillment.

Consider Daniel confessing his sins and the sins of his people right before the angel Gabriel comes to him in swift flight at the time of the evening sacrifice (Daniel 9). In fact, life in the middle is Daniel the day before that and the day before that, praying and showing up with no angel in sight!

Life in the middle is the woman with the issue of blood living faithfully *before* she experiences divine imagination and touches the hem of Jesus' garment (Mark 5:25-34). In her case, it was going from doctor to doctor while at the same time keeping her faith.

Life in the middle is Moses *after* he flees from Pharaoh but *before* he sees the burning bush—a period that lasted forty years (Exodus 2:15-3:1)! Sometimes, it's like Moses looking over into the Promised Land but not being allowed to enter in due to his disobedience, but knowing the love and friendship of God anyway (Deuteronomy 34:1-4).

It's Joseph on any given day during his twenty-three year sojourn to a place of prominence he had no idea he was destined for (Genesis 37:23-41:1). It's Joseph on any ordinary Tuesday morning while in slavery to Potiphar, wondering why, but keeping the faith (Genesis 39:2-6).

Life in the middle is Paul and Silas living faithfully as they are being stripped of their clothes and beaten severely. It's Paul and Silas praying and singing to God at midnight *after* the shackles but *before* the angelic prison break (Acts 16:22-34)!

It's John on the Isle of Patmos *after* being exiled but *before* he has the visions.

It's Habakkuk receiving an entirely different and undesirable answer to prayer but rejoicing anyway (Habakkuk 3:16-19). It's Habakkuk waiting for a vision that tarries (2:3).

It's Jeremiah observing the worst atrocities imaginable during the exile but grabbing hold of a reason to trust God anyway (Lamentations 3:19-26).

It is Hannah in any one of her years of weeping (1 Samuel 1:6-8), *after* realizing she was barren but *before* becoming pregnant with Samuel—still hoping, still praying, with no answer in sight.

It's the man formerly known as Legion living faithfully for Jesus after Jesus leaves (Mark 5:1-20). Free of his demons, he "went away and began to tell in the Decapolis how much Jesus had done for him." (Note: It's good to remember how much Jesus has done for us!)

It's Noah before he hears from God and gets instructions to build the ark. It's Noah in the midst of the years with no rain in sight but building the ark anyway and in spite of the jeers of his neighbors (Genesis 6).

It's Abraham precisely in the seconds when his fingers grabbed hold of the knife to slay his son. It's the faithfulness displayed in that split second when upward momentum gave way to downward thrust before being stopped by the angel (Genesis 22).

It's Job, plagued with boils and "comforters," crying out, "Though he slay me, yet will I hope in him (Job 13:15)!"

It's all those who believe without having had the opportunity to press their fingers into the nail-scarred hands and the riven side of Jesus (John 20:24-29).

It's Simeon and Hannah *before* a couple from Nazareth show up with a newborn in the Temple (Luke 2:22-38).

Life in the middle is every genuine Christian on Monday morning (when the *real* altar call happens) as we respond to the sermon we heard on Sunday by living differently on Monday. It's Monday Christians!

It's a woman going through her daily duties, living faithfully and honoring God *even without fully orchestrated worship music playing in the background!*

It's a man facing the realization that he has failed God yet again, but getting up, confessing his sins, repenting, and struggling forward.

Before moving forward...

We have all seen what happens when you move a large, sedentary rock or piece of wood out of its place. Underneath are all kinds of critters, caught unawares, scrambling around and running for cover. In that moment, we catch them doing whatever it is they do when no one is looking. Life in the middle is sort of like that. It's how we are living in real life when no one is looking! How is that going for *you*, by the way? Before moving forward, out of the examples just shared, pick the one that most inspires you; that best applies to your present situation. Think through it. Imagine what it was like for that person. Try to discover what it was they were holding onto as they faithfully lived their lives in the middle. Is that something that would work for you?

Now, get ready! Because we are about to dive into God's process!

2

God's Process

God has a process. He has a way in which He moves us forward toward His will for our lives and toward participation in the larger story of what He is doing in time and history. This process is essentially characterized by several "movements" or stages.

The flow of the process begins when we are dissatisfied with the status quo in our lives.[1] From this dissatisfaction arises a holy disturbance, a *divine dissatisfaction* if you will, which causes us to reconsider a great many things such as our fruitfulness, our attitudes, our actions, our future, and our purpose, just to mention a few. We begin to feel a spiritual *burden*. Out of this burden flows heartfelt, passionate, effectual *prayer*. This fervent, effectual prayer, fueled by the burden, produces a fresh, new vision—*God's* vision. You could call it *divine imagination!*

The vision can come in more than one way. It can be a direct word from the Lord, revealing His plan, or a simple thought we realize is from God. In any case, it is a picture of what things could be like if there were no barriers.[2] At this point, we must recognize that the vision, which flowed out of prayer, inspires more prayer which ultimately brings the vision to fruition.

In summary, divine dissatisfaction leads to spiritual burden, and burden leads us into fervent, effectual prayer. Prayer gives birth to the vision (*divine imagination*), and then, bathed in further prayer, the vision is realized (*victory*). All that remains is to rejoice at what God has done in participation with us!

Divine Imagination

The clearest pictures of this process can be seen in Scripture in the stories of Hannah (1 Samuel 1) and Habakkuk (Habakkuk 1-3), both of which we will look at in *Part 2*. However, there are many stories in which we are allowed to see parts of the process. Many times, the part we get to see is that part of the process called *divine imagination*.

In the New Testament, divine imagination can be clearly seen in the stories of Bartimaeus (Mark 10:46-52), the healing of the Centurion's servant (Matthew 8:5-13), the woman with the issue of blood (Mark 5:25-34), the prostitute who washes Jesus's feet with her tears (Luke 7:36-50), and even the Syrophoenician woman (Mark 7:24-30). The imagination we see in these stories is most poignant.

Bartimaeus envisioned in his mind's eye that, when the opportunity presented itself, he would cry out to Jesus, appealing to Him as the Son of David, and be healed of his blindness.

The Centurion had it worked out in his mind that Jesus could simply "say the word" and it would be done.

The woman with the issue of blood envisioned an opportunity to touch the hem of Jesus's cloak and imagined that such a touch would bring healing.

The prostitute who washed Jesus' feet with her tears and dried them with her hair envisioned Jesus' acceptance of a daring act of worship that would minister to Him in a powerful way.

The Syrophoenician woman, faced with a racial barrier to her request, imagined a concept that persuaded Jesus, namely, that even the dogs eat crumbs from the Master's table.

If she was a dog in comparison to the Jews, then perhaps she could have just a crumb. She imagined that a crumb would be enough, and she was right! In fact, all of these succeeded at realizing their visions!

The Death of the Vision

Within God's process we can sometimes see clearly what someone has called "the death of the vision."[3] For example, in the life and experience of the young Moses in Egypt, we observe him as he begins to realize who he really is and something of his purpose. He has a vision, born of his own sense of justice, and begins to insert himself into the personal conflicts of his fellow Hebrews and even kills an Egyptian who was mistreating a Hebrew slave (Exodus 2:11-14)! His efforts end in failure and in an increase of their burden. He experiences the death of *his* vision and flees into to the desert. For forty years he is a shepherd in the desert until finally God calls him and reveals to him *His* vision for the deliverance of His people. Moses' vision is *reborn*, but in God's way and according to God's timing.

Habakkuk experienced the death of the vision in some ways. He had a vision of God's justice and he assumed that God would ultimately intervene among His people. God chose to answer Habakkuk's prayer in an entirely different way. After some arguing with God, Habakkuk let go of his vision and embraced God's.

By the time we see Gideon he has already given up on his vision and entered into bitterness and complaint. We watch as he struggles to take hold of God's vision, testing it over and over, before finally trusting it and achieving victory.

Abraham was certainly fully engaged in the process. He actually had embraced God's vision but then grew weary of waiting for it, allowing himself to be influenced by *Sarah's* vision which brought Hagar and Ishmael into the picture. Ishmael represents what can happen when we try to bring a God-given vision to pass with human ingenuity.

Dynamics of Life in the Middle

The study of God's process brings out a number of dynamics vital to successful Christian living. We immediately begin to see that elements such as waiting on the Lord, spiritual warfare, and the mystery of how and why God chooses to partner with us in this way are all integral parts of God's process. We discover that what we call hardship God calls education (Hebrews 12:4-11) and that without trouble we would scarcely ever make it to our divine appointments (see the story of Joseph in Genesis 37-45).

We rejoice when God grants and brings the vision to pass. But once we get to know Him and have begun to understand His process, we realize that the rejoicing begins *before* we see the vision come to pass.4 Why? Because we know His heart and we know that He intends to bring about His vision for our lives. But even more, we rejoice because we have matured to the point that we realize that *He is our portion* (see Chapter 11). We move on from the days of the childish pursuit of selfish desires and ambitions and we embrace the reality that the greatest reward at the end of the day is God Himself! He is our portion! We agree with the writer of Lamentations that, because He is our portion, we can wait patiently for Him! Knowing that He is our portion sustains us in our difficult times and stabilizes us when we prosper.

Ultimately, understanding God's process redirects our gaze to the eternal; to the amazing workings that are going on in the spiritual realm. In effect, it throws back the curtains, allowing us to see some of what goes on in the heavenlies as God condescends to participate with us.

Before moving forward...

So, where are you in God's process? From time to time, I encounter people who are concerned about their lack of spiritual sensitivity or connection to God. They are clearly upset, feeling as though God has rejected or abandoned them. It is a pleasure for me to help them see that the very fact of their worry is evidence of the Holy Spirit's drawing.

Hannah Whitall Smith captures the essence of life in the middle when she describes the lump of clay in the Potter's hands. She said,

> The lump of clay, from the moment it comes under the transforming hand of the potter is, during each day and each hour of the process, just what the potter wants it to be at that hour on that day, and therefore pleases him; but it is very far from being matured into the vessel he intends in the future to make it. . . The apple in June is a perfect apple for June; it is the best apple that June can produce: but it is very different from the apple in October, which is a perfected apple.[5]

Before moving forward, invite God to immerse you into His process, trusting that He will do it and that He will finish the work (Philippians 1:6)!

3

Participating With God:
The "Curtain" Passages

In each of the following passages, which I have come to call "curtain" passages, movement on earth and movement in the heavenlies are bound together. That is, we see God acting in heaven in cooperation with humanity on earth in order to bring about His will. Many times, it is a picture of God's response to His children when they begin to ask for that which He already wants to do. At other times, it reveals God's initiative in inviting His people to participate in what He has decided to do.

These stories are unique because of the human steps that initiate a heavenly response or the human response that comes as a result of heavenly initiation. In each of the stories a unique glimpse at a heavenly process is evident. Sometimes the uniqueness is an outcome dependent on human follow-through. Sometimes it is a glimpse into heavenly timing. At other times it is a glimpse into the strategic moving of spiritual forces both good and evil. At any rate, these stories pull back the curtains and provide a glimpse into heavenly realities and say something to us about the desire for divine-human participation in the heart and will of God.

Moses's Uplifted Hands: The Battle in the Balance (Ex 17:8-13)

In this story we have an account of a particular battle between the Israelites (led by Joshua), and the Amalekites. It would have been a typical battle but something curious happened! The text tells us that "as long as Moses held up his hands, the Israelites were winning" but when Moses would let down his hands the tide would turn and the Amalekites would start winning (Exodus 17:11). So important was it that Moses's hands remain raised that Aaron and Hur found a rock for Moses to sit on and then stood beside him (one on each side) and held his hands up until sunset!

One cautious, unimaginative writer explained that Moses may have been giving signals to the army which helped them win the battle. Most would agree that constantly upheld hands make for a non-descript signal! It is obvious that the story of the upheld staff or rod is told in the context of the miraculous intervention of God seen in the Meribah story. In Exodus 17:6, God tells Moses to strike the rock with his staff. When he does, water comes out. Then, in verse 9, Moses makes a point to tell them that he will be on the top of the hill "with the staff of God in my hand." We are then told specifically that Moses held up his hands. Grounded in the actions seen within the context of the passage, we can easily infer that God is again choosing to do a miracle through Moses with the staff of God in his hands. I call this *grounded inference*.

What was happening behind the curtains? God had determined that as long as Moses held up the staff, the battle would advance in Israel's favor. In this we can see that it was necessary for Moses to cooperate or *participate* with God for when Moses would let down his hands, or the staff, the battle began to go in Amalek's favor (verse 11). A miracle is determined in heaven, but participation is required on earth in order to bring the miracle to pass.

Banging the Arrows for Victory
(2 Kings 13:14-24)

In this story, the evil king Jehoash (v 11) came to the prophet Elisha needing help to obtain a victory over a particular enemy, Aram. The prophet told him to "Get a bow and some arrows . . . take the bow in your hands . . . open the east window . . . and shoot (2 Kings 13:15-17)!" When that happened Elisha cried out, "The Lord's arrow of victory, the arrow of victory over Aram!" and declared to the evil king, "You will completely destroy the Arameans at Aphek." Then, Elisha told him to take the arrows and strike them on the ground (v 18). When the king only struck them to the ground three times, the prophet got angry and announced to Jehoash that he should have stricken the ground five or six times and that he would now *not* have a complete victory but instead that he would defeat Aram only three times (v 18-19).

This passage gives us important insight into a few things. First, we see that the king was pursuing victory through spiritual means. In other words, he consulted the prophet in an effort to elicit help from him. The king obtained a complete victory over his enemy *through spiritual means*. He would still have to fight the enemy with the conventional weapons of the time, but he would be victorious because he had gained a supernatural guarantee of victory through his participation in a spiritual process (thus a picture of spiritual warfare to a certain degree).[6]

Second, his *participation* was needed to complete the process. He was told to strike the ground. Somehow, the act of striking the ground in the proper way was part of the key to victory. A complete victory had been decreed but required the proper response from the king.

Third, we observe that when the king cooperated with the prophet a victory was declared. Of course, the prophet Elisha could not have made that decision on his own, so through the principle of *grounded inference*, we can assume that God decreed the victory in heaven and revealed it to the prophet.[7] God granted the king's desire of a total victory over his enemies but the victory was *contingent* upon the king's cooperation. The victory that *did* ensue was proportionate to the king's participation!

The Servant's Eyes Opened
(2 Kings 6:18)

This passage is fairly easy to unpack and is one of the most direct demonstrations of spiritual warfare in the Bible. When Elisha and his servant had been surrounded by the enemy, the servant panicked and wondered what they would do. Elisha told him, "Don't be afraid, those who are with us are more than those who are with them (2 Kings 6:16)." The servant's eyes were opened and he saw that the hills were full of horses and chariots of fire.

As the curtains are parted, Elisha's servant (and the readers of this story) learn that militant, spiritual forces of heaven array against evil human militant forces. However, through *grounded inference* (taking other passages into consideration such as Daniel 10 and Ephesians 6), we can assume that there were evil *spiritual* militant forces behind the earthly ones as well.

A Delay in the Heavenlies
(Daniel 10:1-14)

In this passage, Daniel is seen fasting and seeking God in order to "gain understanding" and to humble himself before God (Daniel

10:2-3, 12). Three weeks after he began to fast, he encountered a powerful angelic being, likely an archangel.[8] This being informed him that he had been sent from God as soon as Daniel had set his mind to pray and fast, but he had been detained by the Prince of Persia. Since we know that a human prince of Persia would never be able to detain an archangel, we know that the Prince of Persia was the evil spiritual authority over the godless nation and region of Persia. For twenty-one days the archangel tried to press through in order to bring Daniel a word from the Lord but was unsuccessful until Michael the archangel came and helped him (v 13)!

This passage gives us a clear picture of the battle that rages in the heavenlies and how we can be, and are, caught up in it.

The Harbinger Sword (Joshua 5:13-15)

On the eve of the Battle of Jericho, Joshua looked up and saw a man standing in front of him with his sword drawn (Joshua 5:13). As we continue to read, we discover that the "man" was actually the Son of God in His pre-incarnate form, thus making it a theophanic appearance. We know it was a theophanic appearance because Joshua, hearing that this man was "the commander of the army of the Lord," fell down in reverence and was not reprimanded for doing so. Then, the man said to Joshua, "Take off your sandals, for the place where you are standing is holy (v 15)." This was of course reminiscent of Moses's experience with God at the burning bush (Exodus 3).

The salient point for this study is the appearance of a heavenly being, in this case a theophanic appearance of the pre-incarnate Son of God, inserting himself into the human realm. In this case, the "being" was holding a sword. We can surmise that, on the eve of battle, this lifted sword was a picture of God's posture, if you will, in heaven. It was an indication that war had been declared in heaven and that as they entered into battle against Jericho they could expect total victory.

The "Sound of Marching" (2 Samuel 5:17-25)

Another passage demonstrating the importance of humans participating with God and the insertion of heavenly beings into the affairs of men is the story of David and the "sound of marching." In this story, an occasion arises on which there is the potential for a battle between the people of God and the

Philistines. What makes this passage interesting is that, indeed, David consults the Lord before going into battle, thus bringing to bear upon the earthly battle the spiritual resources of God. So, we see a picture of spiritual warfare in its simplest form: praying to God for help. The Lord gave David permission to go, assuring him of a victory. David and Israel went to battle and won a great victory.

Next, we see another opportunity for battle, situated exactly as the first one (same place, same enemy), and yet, when David inquires of the Lord, he receives instruction to fight the second battle differently. In the first battle, David got permission to fight, went forward and fought a traditional battle. In the second, battle, God told David,

> Do not go straight up, but circle around behind them and attack them in front of the balsam trees. As soon as you hear the sound of marching in the tops of the balsam trees, move quickly, because that will mean the Lord has gone out in front of you to strike the Philistine army (2 Samuel 5: 23-24).

David obeyed God, waited to hear "the sound of a going in the tops of the mulberry trees

(KJV)," and the Lord went out in front of him to strike the Philistine army.

Why the difference? Isn't God able to enable David to fight in any situation? Couldn't God have done it the same way both times? Of course, the answer is yes. But the profundity of this story is that, for whatever reason, God chooses to do things one way and then, in seemingly identical circumstances, chooses to do things in a different way, *letting us participate in the process!*

The Demon-Possessed Boy of Mark 9

In Mark 9, Jesus came down from the Mount of Transfiguration only to find that the disciples could not cast a demon out of a young man who was there. The expectation of the people, the disciples, and the father of the demon-possessed boy was that the authority to cast out the demon had already been granted to the disciples. There was reason to expect that the demon would be cast out. But the disciples couldn't do it. When they asked Jesus why, He said, "This kind comes out only by prayer (and fasting in some versions of Scripture; v. 9)." That is, the disciples would have to pray in some particular way other than had already been done in order to cast out a demon like the one encountered. God

40

was willing and indeed authority had been granted, but further participation on the disciples' parts was needed.

Apprehending the Promise

The truths that arise from the concept of God's participation with us are simple, yet profound. God was willing to save a remnant of creation from the flood, but someone would have to build an ark (Genesis 6:5-22). In Exodus 17, He was willing for Israel to win the battle over the Amalekites, but only if Moses continued to hold up his hands and the staff of God. He was willing to let the people cross over the Jordan river into the Promised Land on dry ground, but this time, instead of parting the waters first, as at the Red Sea, the priests would have to "get their feet wet" first, then God would do His part (compare Exodus 14:10-31 with Joshua 3:8-17). Healing was available for Naaman, but first he would have to dip seven times in the Jordan's muddy waters (2 Kings 5:1-14). Hannah can have that baby boy she longs for just as soon as she yields her vision to God's (1 Samuel 1).

Our Remarkable Partnership with God

When you think about it, it is remarkable, this partnership we have with God! We have not seen Him, yet we can hear His voice, know His will, and do on earth what is done in heaven! God delights to see us *complete the circuit* when we, through prayer, begin to do on earth what He has ordained in Heaven. He inspires us to ask Him to do what He was longing to do in the first place!

The insight gleaned from these stories may be a stretch for some. But for those who can receive it, it will be a powerful revelation for their lives. Here it is in a nutshell: God, usually in response to our prayers but always according to *His* timing, reveals from heaven what He has determined to do. And yet, though the blessing has been granted, it must be appropriated through our participation with Him.

Before moving forward...

Pope Benedict XVI wrote:

> The recitation of this prayer. . . "Hear, O Israel: The Lord our God is one LORD..." was understood as the act of taking upon one's shoulders the yoke

of God's sovereign lordship. This prayer is not just a matter of words: the one who prays it accepts God's lordship, which consequently, through the act of praying, enters into the world. The one who is praying helps to bear it on his shoulders, and through his prayer, God's lordship shapes his way of life, his day-to-day existence, making it a locus of God's presence in the world.[9]

What a powerful statement! Did you imagine that your "life in the middle" was a locus of God's presence in the world? That somehow, through your participation with God, in worship, prayer, and obedience, God makes your life a place of His Presence? Before moving forward, take a moment to meditate on that reality. Then, finding a place where you can pray and worship undisturbed, *enjoy* that reality! Thank God for making your life a place of His Presence in the world and ask Him to continue doing so in an even greater way.

Part 2

Hannah and Habakkuk:

Two Lives
Lived in the Middle

Part One laid important ground work for understanding concepts like *divine dissatisfaction*, *divine imagination*, the *death of the vision*, *God's process*, and *participating with God*. In this section, we will observe these concepts up close in the lives of Hannah and Habakkuk.

As you read, take time to feel Hannah's pain and Habakkuk's frustration. Discover whether Elkanah or Peninnah helped Hannah the most. Ask yourself, *How far can one go when questioning God?*

4

Hannah

As the sun comes up on the hill country of Ephraim, somewhere near the end of the twelfth century B.C., we find a young woman living during a particularly lawless period in Israel's history, just as the time of the judges was about to give way to the time of the kings. The young woman's name was Hannah. The precarious nature of the times she lived in is captured in the last verse of the Book of Judges:

> In those days Israel had no king; everyone did as he saw fit (Judges 21:25).

Hannah had no idea the role she would play in bringing about Israel's first king!

Hannah's Situation

The first thing we learn about Hannah is that she is married to a man named Elkanah. The second thing we learn is that she had no children, though she desperately desired them.

It could not have been easy for her, living in those days, living in those times, to negotiate her barrenness with the culture around her. Women were treated little better than property in most cases, but their ability to provide children, particularly sons, increased their value. A *barren* woman would have felt the sting of reproach! She would have been viewed by many as not having been blessed by God, and by others as being specifically cursed by Him.[10]

I would like to hurry on to say that the text does not say that Hannah was barren: it says she had no children. We read barrenness into the story because we quickly observe that Hannah is in great distress over the absence of children in her life and because the situation continues for years. We will make other important observations about this as the story unfolds.

We do not know what Hannah thought of herself or, in her estimation, where God was in relation to her barrenness, but it is likely she felt that something was wrong with her. Perhaps others looked at her as if she were under God's judgment. She probably wondered why God would allow her to go through the agony of being childless. In candid moments she might have said, "Why has God abandoned me?" or simply, "Where is God?" In reality, however, God was intimately involved with Hannah for the Bible tells us that "the LORD had closed her womb (verses 5 and 6)."

Consider Job

Does God close wombs? Some people really struggle with this idea. The same tension arises over Job's suffering. What does the Bible say? One day, when the angels came to present themselves before the LORD, Satan showed up as well. God commended Job to him saying,

> Have you considered my servant Job? There is no one on earth like him; he is blameless and upright, a man who fears God and shuns evil (Job 1:8).

Like it or not, Job's troubles began as a result of his *faithfulness*, though some have argued that Job's troubles came on him because of his *fear*.

> What I feared has come upon me; what I dreaded has happened to me (Job 3:25).

In fact, an entire doctrine has been built upon this Scripture, claiming that if we fear something we will ultimately be doomed to experience it. Have you ever feared something that ultimately did *not* happen to you? Of course you have! In Mark 4:37-40, the disciples were afraid their ship was going to sink and they were going to drown, yet it did not happen. Job is simply stating that something he had always dreaded and hoped would *not* happen to him *did* happen to him. It is important not to ignore Scripture on this point. The fact is that, according to the text, it was not Job's fear that caused his trouble but his *righteousness*. Further, we must admit that God allowed it! We shouldn't ignore or misinterpret Scripture simply because it leaves us with a troubling tension.

Hannah was unable to have children because the Lord had closed her womb (it helps to say it out loud). Consequently, Hannah wept bitterly for years, struggling with the emptiness and the stigma of being barren. And yet it was her bitter weeping and her dissatisfaction with her barrenness that led her to the path God wanted her to take.

If we had our way, we would be delivered this instant of all of our sorrows, troubles, pains, and discomforts. Every time we come together in our church services we ask God to heal the sick, mend the broken hearted, prosper those who are struggling financially, and, in general, to deliver us from all of our troubles. We are not wrong for doing so. In fact, we are told not to "worry about anything; instead, pray about everything. Tell God what you need, and thank him for all he has done (Philippians 4:6, NLT)." Nevertheless, Scripture is clear that one of the most significant methods used by God to motivate and move us in our Christian walk is the pain we endure as a result of our trials. One of the most significant examples of this truth is found in the life of Joseph.

Joseph

Joseph's brothers hated him because he was favored by their father Jacob, and also because he lorded his dreams over them (Genesis 37). So, one day, they threw him into a pit and left him for dead. In fact, they led their father to believe that he had been killed "by a ferocious animal" (verse 33). From the pit Joseph was sold into slavery to a man named Potiphar (v. 36). While a slave in Potiphar's house, he was the object of a false accusation made by Potiphar's seducing wife—an event which landed him in prison (Genesis 39:6-20). Ultimately, he became the most powerful man in Egypt, second only to Pharaoh (Genesis 41:39-40), and was used by God to preserve multitudes from dying in a severe famine, including his father, his brothers, and their families (Genesis 45:4-7).

Twenty-three years passed from the time Joseph was abandoned by his brothers to the pit until the time he ascended to power in Egypt. Although the Bible does not specifically say it, there is no reason to doubt that Joseph, like anyone else would have, had to fight against bitterness in his struggle to understand why God would give him such powerful gifts (his dreams, administrative abilities, etc.) only to be squandered in slavery and prison!

The story of Joseph is the stuff of children's Sunday school stories. Because of this, we have a tendency to overlook the indicators that show us the pain Joseph must have gone through. In Genesis 42:21, we learn that Joseph pleaded for his life when they put him into the pit. In Genesis 40:15, Joseph reveals that he senses the injustice of what had been done to him by his brothers. It is easy to sum up Joseph's life with all-too-convenient alliteration (pit, Potiphar, prison, palace, etc.) and yet leave out an important word: pain!

Joseph had endured the pit, Potiphar's house, the prison, and then ascended to the palace, but then it happened! He received a profound revelation that revealed God's purpose. In Genesis 45:8, while revealing himself to his brothers, Joseph acknowledges a life changing discovery. It was not his brothers who started the chain reaction of events that would send Joseph through twenty-three troubled years: It was God!

> For two years now there has been famine in the land, and for the next five years there will not be plowing and reaping. But God sent me ahead of you to preserve for you a remnant on earth and to save your lives by a great deliverance. *So then, it was not you who sent me here, but God.* He made me father to Pharaoh, lord of his entire household and ruler of all Egypt (Genesis 45:6-8, NIV, emphasis mine).

Back to Hannah

As her story progresses, it becomes obvious to readers of the biblical story that God was intimately involved in what was happening with Hannah. But it wasn't obvious to her. It was God's will for Hannah to become pregnant with a child that would grow up to become the mighty prophet Samuel! But it would take years for Hannah to come to that realization.

Before moving forward...

Before we go deeper into Hannah's story, consider for a moment your own "theology of trouble." Ask yourself this question, "When I experience trouble in my life, is it because God is with me or because I have displeased Him?" Your answer is telling. Unfortunately, many have developed a theology that says the presence of trouble is an indicator of God's rejection. Hebrews 12 says something different.

> In your struggle against sin, you have not yet resisted to the point of shedding your blood. And you have forgotten that word of encouragement that addresses you as sons: "My son, do not

make light of the Lord's discipline, and do not lose heart when he rebukes you, because the Lord disciplines those he loves, and he punishes everyone he accepts as a son." Endure hardship as discipline; God is treating you as sons (Hebrews 12:4-7).

The word *discipline* in the above passage is translated *chastisement* in the KJV. I don't know about you, but for me, that word has negative connotations. Even the word *discipline* can be taken negatively. But the Greek word that lies beneath these English translations is *paideia*. Paideia means, essentially, education or training. Some form of the word is used eight times in Hebrews 12:4-11!

Trouble, or hardship, can come to us for several reasons. It can come because someone around us does something foolish or even intentionally harmful. It can come because *we* do something foolish or harmful! It can come because we have sinned. It can also come as an assault from our archenemy Satan. But sometimes, trouble just comes. The good news is that God intends to use our hardships, however they come, to teach us how to live; to show us how to live our lives in the middle according to the standards of heaven!

> Our fathers disciplined us for a little while as they thought best; but God disciplines us for our good, that we may share in his holiness. No discipline seems pleasant at the time, but painful. Later on, however, it produces a harvest of righteousness and peace for those who have been trained by it (Hebrews 12:10-11).

We are about to see how God used Hannah's hardships to move her forward into His vision. Had Hannah been willing to accept her barrenness she never would have arrived at God's vision for her life. In the mercy of God, He employed the "help" of a provocateur that would age Hannah's dissatisfaction into *divine* dissatisfaction.

5

Hannah and Peninnah

Fortunately for Hannah, she had a husband who loved her. In fact, he seems not to have been bothered by her barrenness (1 Samuel 1:8). Maybe it was because he was an exceptionally nice guy. Maybe it was because he genuinely loved her. Or perhaps it was because he already had *many* children with his *other* wife, Peninnah!

An oft-quoted verse of Scripture says, "Weeping may endure for a night, but joy comes in the morning (Psalm 30:5). In Hannah's case, the weeping lasted much longer than a night! Yes, she was desperate for a child, but her pain was exacerbated by Peninnah, Elkanah's other wife.

All we know about Peninnah is what we read about her in 1 Samuel 1 and what is inferred in chapter 2, and unfortunately the report is not very good! It is plausible that she was Elkanah's first wife—older, and jealous of the favor Elkanah showed to Hannah (1 Samuel 1:5). She had at least four children,[11] though probably more, and, for whatever reason, she was cruel to Hannah. In fact, she was Hannah's rival (v. 6)! When the family would go up to Shiloh to worship, Peninnah would provoke Hannah to irritate her. So sore was Peninnah's provocation that Hannah would ultimately break down in tears and lose her desire to eat!

Year after Year

Tennessee Williams wrote, "Time is the longest distance between two places."[12] The more familiar we become with a particular Bible passage, particularly a narrative passage, the more likely we are to overlook important details, not taking the time, as Dallas Willard says, to "feel the weight others are feeling."[13] In the case of Hannah, we know she had no children and seemed to have no prospect of any children in her future. We know that she was provoked by her rival Peninnah, and that it caused her to weep and lose her appetite. But a closer look at the passage reveals something worth slowing down to ponder.

> . . . her rival kept provoking her in order to irritate her. This went on *year after year* (1 Samuel 1:6-7, emphasis mine).

It's easy for us to gloss over this reality, but Hannah's ordeal covers the span of years!

Twice it is mentioned that the events of the story repeated themselves year after year. Year after year they would go to Shiloh to worship and to sacrifice to God. Year after year Peninnah, Elkanah's other wife who had many children, would provoke Hannah in order to irritate her. Year after year, Elkanah tried to make up for Hannah's barrenness by giving her double portions of the sacrificial meal because he loved her and felt sympathy for her situation. Year after year, Hannah had no appetite because the provocateur would bring her to tears. Year after year Elkanah was confounded at Hannah's profound dissatisfaction. He wondered why having him for a husband was not enough for her. And year after year, Hannah remained barren.

It is a fairly typical human response to view the presence of trouble as the absence of God. I remember growing up, my father tied

God's approval to his financial condition. If things were going well, he could be convinced of God's acceptance of him. If things were bad, it was a sign that God had rejected him.

It is a painful feeling to be in God's house and be barren because the barrenness can begin to seem like God's commentary on your relationship with Him. But when the story is finally told, Hannah's barrenness was *not* punishment from God but rather *His involvement in her life*!

Before moving forward...

It is this period in Hannah's life—somewhere in the middle of years filled with disappointment, confusion, and tears—that we get a taste of the desperate side of life in the middle. It's easy to look at Hannah's story three thousand years after the fact and see what God was doing. But we know from our own experiences that life in the middle can move really slowly!

Before moving forward, consider those around you who this very moment feel trapped in the midst of years filled with anguish. Consider the autistic child who struggles with his or her environment and feels such pain, and the parents who have labored for years under the heavy burden of caring for a child with special needs. Or how about those who feel sick every day or those locked in a prison of bondage that seems impossible to escape? And what about you? Have you given up hope? Don't! God is with us in the middle! I promise you, the truths that are yet to be shared in this little book are life changing! So hang on! Help is on the way! In the meantime, find someone who has been struggling for years and encourage them. Maybe just be with them so that they know they are not alone.

6

Elkanah's "Offer"

Elkanah provided for Peninnah and her children, but he *loved* Hannah (1Samuel 1:5)! He favored her. It would seem that he loved her, provided abundantly for her, and did not value her based on her ability to provide children for him. The fairness of Elkanah's favoritism, or the wisdom of having two wives are perhaps topics for a future discussion. And we might like to ask Elkanah why he allowed Peninnah to continue to harass Hannah? But it is the four questions that Elkanah asks Hannah that are most pertinent to this part of the story, particularly the last one.

> Elkanah her husband would say to her, "Hannah, why are you weeping? Why

> don't you eat? Why are you down-
> hearted? Don't I mean more to you
> than ten sons (1 Samuel 1:8)?"

Some might say that Elkanah's first three questions were just standard fare from another insensitive male. Although I think Elkanah showed himself to be at least somewhat sensitive and caring to Hannah, charges of insensitivity towards Peninnah might gain traction due to his lack of wisdom in giving Hannah double portions. Too many assumptions have to be made to run very far with any of these ideas, though it isn't too far-fetched to see in Elkanah a lack of spiritual sensitivity, a point I will visit again below. However, it's the last question that brings several things to light!

The Replacement Vision

Elkanah's last question is a loaded one. The Bible record gives no indication of Hannah's answer, although the context answers it very clearly. Elkanah asks, "Don't *I* mean more to you than ten sons?" This question places Hannah squarely at a crossroads. In essence, Elkanah is making Hannah an offer: if she wanted to, she could simply choose to accept things as they are, enjoy the favor of a loving husband, and allow *him*, with his "double-portion love," to be a substitute for all the sons and daughters she was desperate for. We don't know the degree to which she considered Elkanah's question at the moment he asked it or the degree to which Hannah herself would have been able to articulate why her answer to his question was "No!"(though it clearly was). All we know is that she couldn't do it. Something would not let her! She simply could not shake her desperation to have a child!

Perhaps Elkanah's question indicated his own awareness that Hannah's grieving had gone beyond what was normal for a "barren" woman. Something else was going on! Perhaps Elkanah's question even helped Hannah begin to realize that her dissatisfaction was indeed *divine* dissatisfaction!

One more thing about Elkanah—he did not know what God was doing in Hannah's life but, because of his love for her, he inadvertently offered her a *replacement* vision, which is frequently the case with the Elkanah's of the world. They essentially become dream killers because they themselves do not seem to pick up on divine imagination. Because of the deficiency in their own vision, they tend to dismiss the visions of others.

Elkanah was not the answer to Hannah's emptiness. When Abraham was in the midst of God's process, God spoke to him and said, "I am . . . your very great reward (Genesis 15:1, NIV)." Only God and *His* vision would be able to fill Hannah's empty place.

Barren or Unfruitful?

As was mentioned above, the Bible does not refer to Hannah as barren. Prior to my study of Hannah, I always saw her story as one of a woman who was broken-hearted because she was barren. But it dawned on me that she was not barren, she just hadn't borne fruit yet. There is something important in that thought for our personal lives and our churches.

Many Christians and churches are not bearing fruit. Is it because they are barren or is it that they simply have not borne fruit yet? Time will tell whether they will grow comfortable with not bearing fruit, thus becoming unfruitful, or whether they will allow their dissatisfaction with unfruitfulness to bring them into God's vision for their lives and the lives of their churches.

A. W. Tozer, referring to the Apostle Peter, wrote, "There was a man once who followed the Lord afar off. But he couldn't live with it. Some of you have learned to live with it."[14] Are we unfruitful because we have settled into a Christian lifestyle that accepts the absence of God's manifestation and the fruit that comes with His presence and power? Or are we still open to the leading of divine dissatisfaction? In divine dissatisfaction, God uses our sense of emptiness, or barrenness, or the pain we feel in our trials, to help us divinely imagine things differently, "pray in" the reality of that divinely imagined life, and to learn how to participate with Him (Chapters 2 & 3).

Divine Dissatisfaction

Everyone has problems. In Eliphaz the Temanite's opinion, "Man is born to trouble as surely as sparks fly upward (Job 5:7)." Sometimes trouble is just trouble. But sometimes God uses our trouble to bring about something we had not considered. Hannah was not simply experiencing dissatisfaction. She was experiencing *divine* dissatisfaction brought on by the death of her vision.

Baby Eagles

Frances Hamerstrom, observing baby eagles in the wild,[15] noticed that as young eagles mature and become ready for flight, their parents feed them less and less.

> A parent flew by, downwind, dangling a young marmot in its feet. The eaglet almost lost his balance in his eagerness for food. Then the parent swung by again, closer, upwind, and riding the updraft by the eyrie [nest], as though daring him to fly. Lifted light by the wind, [the eaglet], flying—or more gliding—for the first time in his life. He sailed across the valley to make a scrambling, almost tumbling landing on a bare knoll. As he turned to get his bearings the parent dropped the young marmot nearby. Half running, half flying he pounced on it, mantled [spreading its wings in order to cover its captured prey], and ate his fill.[16]

The baby eagle has for all its life been fed by its parents, dwelled in safety, and wanted for nothing. You could say its "dream" or "vision" is that such an arrangement would continue on perpetually. Its parents, however, know that it is meant for so much more. They are not content to continue to feed the baby into its adulthood for the rest of its life. It must discover its higher purpose! So, mama begins to feed the eaglet just enough to keep it alive, but for the most part, allows the baby to endure the discomfort of hunger so that it will be inspired to leap out and discover abilities and purposes it had never imagined or experienced before!

Most of us have a lot in common with the baby eagle. We settle. We get comfortable. Our thinking and our vision narrows. Even if we read the Bible and pray regularly, we are still unable to see the bigger picture of what is possible with God! So, what does God do? He allows us some discomfort. He allows us to experience *divine dissatisfaction*. He wants to do something remarkable in our lives but we won't be able to see it as long as life barrels along, unhindered by any difficulties.

Let me emphasize that not every difficulty is due to the death of a vision, nor is every trial tied to some drastic change God is trying to implement in your life. He may or may not want you to quit your job and move to Hawaii! Sometimes we suffer a loss or endure a hardship, and always God uses our trials to teach us (Hebrews 12). But *sometimes* our struggles are a prelude to something profound—*divine dissatisfaction leading to divine imagination!!*

How do we know this is the process Hannah was in? Up through verse 8, all we know is that Hannah is childless and distraught, and that the process has gone on for years. Oh, and we know one other thing: **God was**

involved! Verse 5 says, "...and *the Lord* had closed her womb (emphasis mine)." In fact, verses 5 and 6 taken together paint an interesting picture. Because the Lord had closed her womb, Elkanah gave her double portions of the meat when they worshipped at Shiloh, but, for the same reason, Peninnah, her rival, kept provoking her in order to irritate her.

What's the difference between dissatisfaction and *divine* dissatisfaction? Divine dissatisfaction is the pain generated by the death of the vision we had for our lives. It is *divine* because God uses it to call us to a different vision—His! There may be any number of ways that a person whose vision is dying may try to revive it or force it to work or even replace it with something else—even with Elkanah's offer! Dissatisfaction becomes divine dissatisfaction when God uses it to lead us to a new vision and when we allow it to lead us into deep, effectual prayer, which invites God into the situation.

Who is the good guy here?

Isn't it interesting that Elkanah, whom we normally see in a positive light because he tries to console Hannah, is actually, in one sense, the antithesis of what God is doing? Taken to its limits, Elkanah would have Hannah reassess her life, consider his "double-portion love," and be satisfied. Peninnah, on the other hand, whom we normally see in a negative light because of the misery she causes Hannah, is the very person God uses to provoke Hannah to prayer and openness to a new thing that God wants to do, not only in her life, but in the nation of Israel! Much like Joseph's brothers, who threw Joseph into the pit, launching him on a twenty-three year journey to a destiny he never would have reached otherwise, Peninnah is used to provoke Hannah to divine imagination! This does not justify the actions of Peninnah, Joseph's brothers, or any other person God allows to provoke us. But if God uses people like this to move us forward to our destinies, just how angry can we really be at them?

Divine Absurdity

So why did God go to the trouble of closing Hannah's womb in order to bring forth a mighty prophet? The question alone emphasizes a divine absurdity. In order to bring about the birth of a mighty prophet, God closes the womb of the woman who is to give birth to him. We discover that much more is going on in Hannah's life than dissatisfaction over barrenness. Hannah was not only experiencing the normal desire of a woman to have children before her "biological clock" stopped ticking, but she was experiencing the divine dissatisfaction that sets in when our vision runs contrary to God's vision. *God was calling forth Samuel from Hanna's womb!* It was His plan. But this child had to be so prayed for, so clearly from God, that its mother would happily agree to give the child back to God and surrender him to God's calling at such a young age!

> Oh, the depth of the riches of the wisdom and knowledge of God! How unsearchable his judgments, and his paths beyond tracing out! "Who has known the mind of the Lord? Or who has been his counselor?" "Who has ever given to God, that God should repay him?" For from him and through him and to him are all things. To him be the glory forever! Amen (Romans 11:33-36).

The Death of the Vision

Though we have no daily account of it, it is certain that Hannah was driven to her knees in prayer as she dealt with the pain of the divine dissatisfaction she was experiencing. That's what divine dissatisfaction is designed to do. It leads us to prayer. We may ask God, "Why?" We may continue on asking God to bring *our* hopes and dreams to fruition. But when that doesn't happen, we experience the *death of the vision*. What vision? The vision we had for our lives before divine dissatisfaction set in.

Simply put, if our own vision for our lives is not surrendered to God, *His* vision for our lives will not come to pass! Like any other woman aspiring to become a mother, Hannah was looking forward to loving, raising, and nurturing a child. The child would be born, taken care of, taught the family business perhaps, and grow up in the presence of his or her parents, and someday leave the home to start a family of his or her own. This was Hannah's vision. Pretty typical stuff for lives lived in the middle. But because God's vision for Hannah and her progeny was different than Hannah's, God prevented her from experiencing *her* vision so that she would become open to *His* vision. Thus Hannah experienced the *death* of her vision. Like the baby eagle, if God does not allow Hannah to experience divine dissatisfaction, she will never discover *His* vision for her life. The same is true for you and me!

The Rebirth of the Vision

The death of Hannah's vision left her broken and open. Then—it happened! One year, while worshipping with the family at Shiloh, Hannah experienced the birth of the vision— *God's* vision!

> Once when they had finished eating and drinking in Shiloh, Hannah stood up. Now Eli the priest was sitting on a chair by the doorpost of the LORD's temple. In bitterness of soul Hannah wept much and prayed to the LORD. And she made a vow, saying, "O LORD Almighty, if you will only look upon your servant's misery and remember me, and not forget your servant but give her a son, then I will give him to the LORD for all the days of his life, and no razor will ever be used on his head (1 Samuel 1:9-11)."

It took years for Hannah's vision to die. Then, one year, while at Shiloh worshipping the LORD with her family, Hannah had a new thought; an epiphany of sorts. She thought to herself, *I will promise the LORD that, if He will give me a son, I will give the boy back to Him to serve Him all the days of his life.* After experiencing the death of her own vision, she experienced the birth of a new one. This time, it was a vision inspired by God!

God wanted a prophet. He could have simply called anyone He wanted, but God doesn't always do it that way. Instead, He chooses to inspire us to pray for that which He wants to do. Divine imagination becomes reality when we finally ask God to do what He has been wanting to do all along! Why does God bother? He could have accomplished this without Hannah! If He had wanted a prophet he could have just called her son once he was of age. But God desired to partner with Hannah in what He was doing in Israel and in the heavenlies! Hannah never would have thought to make this promise to God without the years of pain!

The Vision Comes to Pass

Hannah's dreams came to pass and she rejoiced greatly (you can read her rejoicings in 1 Samuel 2:1-10). Every year, Hannah would make a new robe for Samuel and bring it to him in the temple. You might think it was hard for Hannah to see Samuel and leave him all over again. No doubt she battled with mixed emotions when she saw Samuel: proud of him, thankfulness to God, still wishing she could have him to herself but also remembering her vow. But, she couldn't stay focused on Samuel for long because as time went by she gave birth to three more sons and two daughters (1 Samuel 2:18-21)!

Gods plan was consummated. If we fast forward to 1 Samuel 3, we discover a little boy who hears Gods voice:

> The boy Samuel ministered before the LORD under Eli. In those days the word of the LORD was rare; there were not many visions. One night Eli, whose eyes were becoming so weak that he could barely see, was lying down in his usual place. The lamp of God had not yet gone out, and Samuel was lying down in the temple of the LORD, where the ark of God was. Then the LORD called Samuel. Samuel answered, "Here I am." And he ran to Eli and said, "Here I am; you called me." But Eli said, "I did not call; go back and lie down." So he went and lay down. Again the LORD called, "Samuel!" And Samuel got up and went to Eli and said, "Here I am; you called me." "My son," Eli said, "I did not call; go back and lie down." Now Samuel did not yet know the LORD: The word of the LORD had not yet been revealed to him. The LORD called Samuel a third time, and Samuel got

up and went to Eli and said, "Here I am; you called me." Then Eli realized that the LORD was calling the boy. So Eli told Samuel, "Go and lie down, and if he calls you, say, 'Speak, LORD, for your servant is listening.' " So Samuel went and lay down in his place. The LORD came and stood there, calling as at the other times, "Samuel! Samuel!" Then Samuel said, "Speak, for your servant is listening." And the LORD said to Samuel: "See, I am about to do something in Israel that will make the ears of everyone who hears of it tingle."

What an amazing picture of God's process and His participation in a simple life being lived faithfully in the middle!

Before moving forward...

How amazing God is! I hope this chapter brought you to a place of awe and wonder at the surprising and wonderful way God works. Before moving forward, think through a couple of things. First, what area of your life can you identify as being genuinely God's vision for your life? How did you discover that? When you look back on that process of discovery, what amazing things did God do, perhaps like He did with Hannah, to show you

His plan for your life? Second, are there some areas of dissatisfaction in your life? Don't assume that those things indicate a massive change, but if you have been stumped for a while, wondering where God is, maybe consider, prayerfully and with godly counsel, whether or not He is trying to redirect you in some way. But be prepared! When God does finally move, you will have to be ready to adjust and move forward with Him! In the next chapter we will see how Habakkuk handled just such a situation.

7

Habakkuk

What is most important in the story of Habakkuk, particularly as it pertains to God's process, is his adjustment to God's vision. He has a burden for what needs to happen in Judah. The wicked of Judah are perpetrating violence and injustice upon the righteous. Habakkuk earnestly prays for God to come and make things right. Divine dissatisfaction sets in when God does not answer quickly enough for Habakkuk's taste. He presses in with his complaint to God—*How long, O Lord?*—until finally, the answer comes. When the answer *does* come, Habakkuk is in disbelief. He becomes disillusioned. God is going to raise up an unrighteous nation (Babylon) and use them to correct Judah! Again he complains to God:

> Your eyes are too pure to look on evil;
> you cannot tolerate wrong. Why then
> do you tolerate the treacherous? Why
> are you silent while the wicked swallow
> up those more righteous than them-
> selves (Habakkuk 1:13)?

God Answers

After making this second complaint to
God, Habakkuk purposes in his heart to wait
for an answer from the Lord,

> I will stand upon my watch, and set me
> upon the tower, and will watch to see
> what he will say unto me, and what I
> shall answer when I am reproved
> (Habakkuk 2:1, KJV).

What comes next is profound in its simplicity.
Habakkuk writes, "And the LORD answered
me . . . (v. 2, ESV)" When the Lord answers us
it may or may not be what we were expecting
or what we had hoped for. But *any* word from
the Lord is nourishing, sustaining, and inspiring. All of Habakkuk's complaints (though not
his concerns) melted away when God revealed
the vision to him:

Write down the revelation and make it plain on tablets so that a herald may run with it. For the revelation awaits an appointed time; it speaks of the end and will not prove false. Though it linger, wait for it; it will certainly come and will not delay. See, he is puffed up; his desires are not upright— but the righteous will live by his faith... (Habakkuk 2:2-4).

God called Habakkuk into participation with Him by instructing him to do three things. He told him to *write down* the revelation or vision so that a herald may run with it. He told him to *wait* for the vision, even if it lingered, because it was certain. In fact, it would at times seem like it was not going to happen at all but, when the time was right, God promised it would. Finally, he told Habakkuk to *live by his faith*. This latter is the battle cry for all those who live purposefully in the middle.

The Vision

We don't get all the details about the vision. We can tell that it is not *local*. That is, it is not simply a vision meant to satisfy Habakkuk's complaints. It is a vision that encompasses the entire earth; all of humanity. It's not just about Judah, but it is about what God is doing and going to do among the nations. The time is coming when "the earth will be filled with the knowledge of the glory of the LORD, as the waters cover the sea." The vision "speaks of the end (Habakkuk 2:3)."

Witness that we are still waiting on this vision to fully come to pass! We are blessed to live on this side of the Incarnation, the crucifixion, and the Resurrection, so we have seen a good deal more than what Habakkuk was allowed to see. But we await the vision to fully come to pass. But it *is* coming. There *will* come a day when the earth will be filled with the knowledge of the glory of the Lord as the waters cover the sea!

God on His Throne

As I was growing up in the church, a common word of encouragement reminded us that, "God is still on His throne!" This is exactly what God was saying to Habakkuk when he asked rhetorically,

> Of what value is an idol, since a man has carved it? Or an image that teaches lies? For he who makes it trusts in his own creation; he makes idols that cannot speak. Woe to him who says to

wood, "Come to life!" Or to lifeless stone, "Wake up!" Can it give guidance? It is covered with gold and silver; there is no breath in it. But the LORD is in his holy temple; let all the earth be silent before him (Habakkuk 2:18-20).

In essence, God has answered Habakkuk and said, "I have heard your complaints. You may not understand my ways but I promise you the day is coming when the whole earth will be filled with the knowledge of the glory of God. It will happen! At times it may seem like the vision has stalled or that it is taking too long. But wait for it: it will come to pass. Meanwhile, live by faith and remember that the Lord is in His holy temple (Habakkuk 2:20)!

In the Midst of the Years

Habakkuk heard God's word and he applied it to his heart. In chapter three of the book of Habakkuk, he pens what is perhaps the best description of the tension that exists between promise and fulfillment for those living faithfully in the middle when he writes,

LORD, I have heard the report about you *and* I fear. O LORD, revive your

> work in the midst of the years, in the midst of the years make it known; in wrath remember mercy (Habakkuk 3:2, NASV).

Stretched by the tension between what theologians have called the *already* and the *not yet*, Habakkuk invites God to show His power, to do His work, and to remember mercy. Habakkuk understood what it meant to live life in the middle.

Divine Enablement

There is one more priceless lesson we learn from Habakkuk's experience. In chapter three of Habakkuk, we get a glimpse of his divine imagination. He is thinking through what it will be like when God finally consummates the vision and brings judgment to the unrighteous and makes all things right (verses 3-15). But then, he comes back to himself and his times and makes a profound statement of faith which takes into account the suffering of the present moment (or at least that which he anticipates is about to descend upon Judah) and God's admonition to live by faith. It is a glimpse of what he felt like when he got the word from God about Babylon, but it is also a picture of how God's vision sustains even in the worst of times.

> I heard and my inward parts trembled, at the sound my lips quivered. Decay enters my bones, and in my place I tremble. Because I must wait quietly for the day of distress, for the people to arise *who* will invade us. Though the fig tree should not blossom and there be no fruit on the vines, *though* the yield of the olive should fail and the fields produce no food, though the flock should be cut off from the fold and there be no cattle in the stalls, yet I will exult in the LORD, I will rejoice in the God of my salvation. The Lord GOD is my strength, and He has made my feet like hinds' *feet,* and makes me walk on my high places (Habakkuk 3:16-19).

In the midst of the years, as he waits quietly for Babylon to come and destroy Judah, Habakkuk discovers that God is there, in the middle, enabling him to rejoice; enabling him to walk on high places! Life lived faithfully in the middle between the promise and its fulfillment is not a life lived alone but rather one lived in the presence of God and in participation with Him! It is a life of purpose based on

God's vision of the present and the future.

Before moving forward...

I have noticed that people struggle with middle existence. We crave closure. At least Hannah eventually experienced the fulfillment of the vision God birthed into her. Not Habakkuk. He would have to live by faith knowing God's plan but not seeing it come to pass. 1 Peter 1:10 says the prophets (like Habakkuk) "searched intently and with the greatest care" to try and figure out when God's promises would finally be consummated. It goes on to say that "even angels long to look into these things." That's the tension that exists in the middle! We know what's coming and we are hungry for it, but for now, we eagerly await its arrival.

For this reason, it is important that we learn how to wait on the Lord.

Part 3

Waiting on the Lord

In chapter one, we took a lightning fast overview of some lives lived in the middle. For instance, we said,

> Life in the middle is Moses *after* he flees from Pharaoh but *before* he sees the burning bush—a period that lasted forty years (Exodus 2:15-3:1)!

Here we can see that forty years passed between Moses' failed attempt to help his people and God's call to him from the burning bush. We didn't take time to imagine what those forty years were like. Was there a crisis of faith? Did he feel abandoned? Sidelined? Were they years of regret? Did he sense that in some way those years were preparing him for what was coming? Did he think *anything* was coming?

In chapters 4-7, we looked in depth at the lives of Hannah and Habakkuk, trying to get a sense of the pain they felt and the way God was leading them. We looked at their situations in a narrative fashion, hearing their stories, but not really examining the specifics of their respective approaches to God.

In these final chapters, we will discuss some of the mechanics of successful living in the middle. These so-called mechanics will be discussed in light of their connection to the larger overall topic of *waiting on the Lord*. The premise of this last section of the book is that meaningful "middle living" is fueled by, and finds its impetus in, learning how to successfully wait on the Lord.

8

Waiting on the Lord

Ever been in the midst of a trial, wondering why God has not answered your prayers and delivered you from your troubles?[17] Having exhausted your creative ability to fix your own problems, you sought for godly council from a fellow Christian (presumably one wiser, more mature), only to hear four undesirable words: *"Wait on the Lord."* Not what you wanted to hear in the midst of your darkest hour! Such advice can seem like a platitude or even a call to do nothing!

Why We Don't Like Waiting!

Let's discuss our distaste for waiting in general. There are at least three reasons we don't like to wait: *impatience, control,* and *desperation.*

Impatience

I am not aware of any situation in which I have waited for something just for the simple joy of waiting. I have waited for things because of the joy of what I knew would happen once the wait was over and I had gotten what I wanted. I have looked back and said, "It was worth the wait" or "I am glad I waited." But waiting, as a chosen activity in lieu of having what I want right now, does not come naturally to me. In fact, it is hard to imagine anything we ordinarily have to wait for that, if given the ability to do so, we wouldn't rather have immediately instead.

Let's be honest! We crave, and are accustomed to, instant gratification. We want to Google it now and get it by the end of the day! When we can't have *what* we want *when* we think we need it or deserve it, it raises questions: "Why can't I have what I want right now?" "Am I not going to get what I want?" "Who's keeping me from getting what I want?" "What can I do to make sure I get what I want?" "How can I speed up the process?" Our discomfort with waiting goes deeper than the desire for instant gratification. It's about *control.*

Control

Les Parrott III, in his book called *The Control Freak*, defines a control freak as a person "who cares more than you do about something."[18] I am less certain about that. That suggests that needing to be in control is all about caring and passion, which I don't believe is true. Control issues are driven by selfishness and insecurity.

When I want something I can't have, it presents a problem. In that moment I must decide how I will handle the news that, for some reason, some force is keeping me from having what I want. Now that "force" could be a chaotic situation, a bureaucratic system, even a specific individual. This becomes a control issue because, by definition, my desire, if strong enough, has the potential to bring about anxiety when it clashes with a force that withholds from me what I want. The controlling attitude says, "I know what is best for me. I can make my own decisions." When that attitude runs into a materialistic/selfish requirement of instant gratification, a perfect storm of frustration, anger, despair—you name it—can arise in a hurry! Why? Human nature is such that each person is convinced that he or she is able to decide for themselves what is best. Even if we don't claim to know what is best for ourselves, we certainly know how to express what we want!

Having to wait for something we passionately desire to have is a glaring indication that we are *not* in control. If we *were* in control we would immediately do what was necessary to get what we want. Why? Because we *really* want it! If we are not in control, and cannot immediately get what we are desperate for, then either *someone else* is in control (hindering us, moving too slowly for our taste, or just plain not caring for our interests), or there is chaos. If there is chaos, we may begin to feel afraid and threatened, and, in the absence of someone in charge, we may engage in the dubious American virtue of stepping up and taking control of our own destinies! If, however, someone else has the upper hand in our circumstances, how can we be sure that things will end well for us or that our best interests will be considered? If we are forced to give up control to another, how can we be sure that that person can be trusted and will treat us with favor? What if I am forced to wait on someone—God for example—who may decide that I do not really need the thing I am desperate for! For these concerns and more, we stand ready to act on our own behalf in order to ensure the outcome.

Desperation

Not every frustration about waiting is due to impatience or a controlling nature. Sometimes we are simply desperate and broken. It is not selfish to long for the healing of a loved one. It is not selfish to want a job so that the family home is not lost. Hannah wasn't selfish for wanting a child, nor was Habakkuk for wanting God to correct the sins of His people. And yet those who long for these noble and important things are frequently called on to wait.

But waiting *on the Lord* is a different reality than the common secular variety of waiting. Every Christian experiences godly delays, but *how* we experience them makes all the difference. Do we enter times of waiting on the Lord kicking and screaming, or do we recognize them as important parts of our walk with God? Is it possible to view waiting on the Lord as something beneficial, even preferred?

Waiting on the Lord

What it Isn't

Waiting on the Lord is often seen as that indefinable, passive state in which beleaguered Christians find themselves wringing their hands in desperation, hoping things turn out right, bereft of any recourse other than to sit and wait, assailed by doubt, confusion, and fear. Helpless Christians in this supposed dilemma are at the mercy of God, whom they admittedly do not know very well, and who may or may not resolve things to their personal satisfaction.

But this is not the biblical description of waiting on the Lord. Waiting on the Lord is not meant to be a ceremonial, religious exercise engaged in while waiting for human machinations and manipulation to take effect; a passive, last-resort, late-hour choice made after exhausting our own abilities and resources. Nor is it one out of many exercises designed to hedge our bets in case we fail to handle things ourselves. The admonition to wait on the Lord is more than empty spiritual jargon. On the contrary, waiting on the Lord is the approach we should take *regardless of the availability of other options*. It is the primary posture of mature Christians, whether or not they are in trouble.[19]

What it Is

Qavah. The very essence of life in the middle is captured in the Hebrew word *qavah*, which means "to wait for eagerly, patiently, hoping, expecting, enduring."[20]

> The word is used to signify depending on and ordering activities around a future event...The hopes of someone can remain unfulfilled, especially when a person or a nation is sinning...Hoping, however, for what God has promised will not ultimately be disappointed, although it may not appear to succeed in the short run...Because He is all-powerful...He will eventually bring His promises to pass.[21]

Four particular Old Testament passages bring out the importance of waiting on the Lord while living faithfully in the middle. The first comes from Psalm 130:

> Out of the depths I cry to you, O Lord; O Lord, hear my voice. Let your ears be attentive to my cry for mercy.
>
> If you, O Lord, kept a record of sins, O Lord, who could stand? But with you there is forgiveness; therefore you are feared.

> I wait for the Lord, my soul waits, and in his word I put my hope. My soul waits for the Lord more than watchmen wait for the morning, more than watchmen wait for the morning.
>
> O Israel, put your hope in the Lord, for with the Lord is unfailing love and with him is full redemption. He himself will redeem Israel from all their sins (NASB).

This Psalm says something to us about *God's heart of love and forgiveness*. It says something about the posture of *waiting on the Lord based on hope in His word*. It captures something of the hopeful desperation we experience as we wait for God to act.

Proverbs 20:22 addresses the releasing of our control mechanisms when it says,

> Do not say, "I will repay evil"; Wait for the Lord, and He will save you (NASB).

Perhaps the most well-known passage concerning waiting on the Lord comes from Isaiah 40:

> Yet those who wait for the Lord will gain new strength; they will mount up

with wings like eagles, they will run
and not get tired, they will walk and
not become weary (NASB).

This passage, while addressing the strength
that comes from waiting on the Lord, also
speaks of being active. The time comes when
we "mount up... run... [and] walk."

Finally, Hosea 12:6 affirms our claim that
waiting on the Lord should be our primary
posture before the Lord:

Therefore, return to your God, observe
kindness and justice, and wait for your
God continually (NASB).

The Hebrew word (tamiyd) lying beneath the
English word *continually* means just that:
"perpetually, always, continually."

In reality, waiting on the Lord is a bold
move; a militant stance; a strategic plan; an
intentional yielding of our will in favor of His
will; a relinquishing of our control (which is
really just self-dependence) and a casting
away of our dependence upon others, in favor
of trusting the Lord to bring about His will. It
is an embracing of God's will instead of our
own; a trusting that God knows our situation,
wants what is best for us (based on *His* definition of "best"), and is actively working on our

behalf. Waiting on the Lord is a ceasing of our labors in favor of resting in Him and trusting Him with the outcome. Now, why wouldn't we want to do that?!

Waiting as resting. The writer of Hebrews talks about Christians entering into God's rest.

> There remains, then, a Sabbath-rest for the people of God; for anyone who enters God's rest also rests from his own work, just as God did from his (Hebrews 4:9-10).

To rest from our own work leaves space for God to do what only He can do. We understand this principle when it comes to salvation. We agree that we cannot save ourselves and that, in order to receive the free gift of eternal life, we must trust in the Lord. But the same can be said about every day of life that follows after salvation. The grace and faith necessary for salvation are also needed in every area of our daily lives. We must trust God with every day, every breath, every decision, every challenge, every blessing. Just as we could not save ourselves, neither can we successfully navigate through the trials or even the blessings we experience each day without God at the helm.

So, waiting on the Lord, properly understood, is a primary, strategic act of surrender, and the only means whereby we may cease from our own labors (and all the efforts we used to engage in as we went about trying to "make our own luck") in favor of trusting God to work on our behalf in each situation.

So, what is it like to wait on the Lord? What does one do while waiting? It may be helpful to view waiting on the Lord as a spiritual discipline.

Waiting as spiritual discipline. According to Dallas Willard, if something is considered to be a spiritual discipline it must be "an activity of mind and body, done to bring our whole selves into cooperation with the divine order, so we can experience more and more a vision and power beyond ourselves."[22] Waiting on the Lord meets that criterion.

Richard Foster teaches us that "every Discipline has its corresponding freedom."[23] He goes on to point out that it is not the discipline we are after but its corresponding freedom.[24] So, what is the corresponding freedom that comes from learning to wait on the Lord? Perhaps one of the freedoms is freedom from our own controlling nature; freedom to trust God; freedom to nurture a lifestyle that purposes to release control to Christ. Ultimately, the freedom to act in participation with God according to His will.

At the very least, waiting on the Lord is the milieu in which spiritual disciplines flourish. It is one thing to find ourselves unhappily stranded in a situation, feeling desperate and forced to pray, and quite another for prayer to rise before the Lord out of a posture of patiently waiting on Him, knowing that it is the means whereby we release into our circumstances our most potent weapon: a loving God who stands ready to do what is best for us *if* we will allow it.

So we can view life as an indecipherable maze of struggles and interruptions where we frequently have to roll up our sleeves and "make our own luck," or we can recognize the divine order in things and realize that waiting on the Lord is the key to releasing God into our situations and circumstances.

Before moving forward...

There are a number of principles necessary for us to grasp if we are to fully benefit from waiting on the Lord as described in this chapter. But first, we must fully grasp the concept of waiting on the Lord as an intentional action and not passive resignation or an unfortunate dilemma. Paradoxically, one of the most powerful things we can do today to move forward in progress is to wait on the Lord! Another divine absurdity? Perhaps.

To move forward from here, we must answer *three foundational questions* concerning the trustworthiness of God. But, before that, there is something even more foundational to successful waiting on the Lord. And that is making the connection between waiting on the Lord and worldview.

9

What Does Worldview
Have to Do With It?

To effectively wait on the Lord we must operate according to a biblical Christian worldview. An explanation of this idea is forthcoming. But first, what *is* a *worldview*?

Our worldview is the philosophical, spiritual perspective from which we answer life's big questions (*Does God exist? What is truth? Is there such a thing as evil? Is there an afterlife?*) and questions concerning human origins. It is the gauge on the reservoir from which we answer the age-old questions *What is the good? What is the good life?* It explains the way we determine wrong or right and how some have decided that there are no such things. The way we determine what is true or false and how some find a way to discount such concepts. It explains the way in which we determine why we did what we did and how we decide what we will do next. It is an indicator of how we tend to process what has been done to us and how we should respond. Our worldview shapes how we look at things and yet has itself been shaped by the things we have seen. We cannot decide simply to have no worldview for that in itself is a way of dealing with the world and is based on some perception of it. Everyone has a worldview.

A genuine biblical Christian worldview is derived from the Bible and supported by a belief—a conviction—that the words written there are God's words and that they describe not only the world we can see but a world we cannot see except our eyes be opened. It answers the questions of life: how we got here, who put us here, and where we are headed. It paints a grand picture of heaven and hell, angels and demons, God and man, life and death.

At first glance, it may not be obvious why a biblical Christian worldview is important for effectively waiting on the Lord, but it concerns our expectations. If we do not understand what the Bible has to say about God's nature, character, purpose, and plan for us, we will formulate and base our expectations of Him on faulty information. Then, in the heat of our trials, we will expect God to act in ways incongruent with His nature. When that happens, we will become discouraged, even disillusioned (see the next chapter), because we will not have understood who God is or what we can rightly expect from Him.

We can more effectively wait upon the Lord when we know God's heart and His purpose for our lives. If we are to relinquish control it is immensely encouraging to know that the one to whom we are yielding can be trusted! That He cares for us and wants what is best for us! (A word of caution here: God's definition of what is good and what is best frequently varies from *our* definition of those ideas!) Therefore, our biblical Christian worldview helps us view, not only the world, but also our experiences in the world in the context of God's eternal purposes, and helps us bring all the resources of heaven to bear upon our circumstances. Having a genuine biblical Christian worldview also helps us understand the nature of spiritual things and how those things drive the world and our experiences in the world. It pulls back the curtains and allows us to see the machinery of heaven.

Before moving forward...

Outside of a biblical Christian worldview we have no framework for understanding God's process as we have described it in this book. We certainly would never be open to the "curtain" passages! Life in the middle, lived faithfully between promise and fulfillment, requires that we believe in God, accept the Bible as the authentic record of His divine self-revelation, and that we give God and His word final authority over our lives. If you have done these three things, you are ready for the three important questions that are coming next.

10

Three Big Questions

Waiting on the Lord comes down to trust: placing the outcome of our lives completely in the hands of God, not interfering or interjecting our own control, willing to accept the outcome without resentment or bitterness.[25] How many people in your life do you trust to that degree? Not many I imagine. Most of us carry around a considerable amount of emotional baggage—a common byproduct of misplaced trust. So, it is understandable if trusting others is not high on our to-do list. But as Christians we have been called to completely and fully trust God.

Three questions beg to be asked here: *Can God be trusted? What can He be trusted to do? Do we trust Him?* The effectiveness with which we are able to wait on the Lord is bound up in the answers to these questions. Before addressing them, however, it will be important first to consider the concept of *disillusionment*.

Why disillusionment?

The reason it is important to discuss the concept of disillusionment before considering the three big questions is to stress how important it is that we answer them correctly. If we fail to get a realistic picture of what the Bible *really* says about God's trustworthiness and what He has *actually* promised, we leave ourselves open to disillusionment.

What is disillusionment?

Disillusionment happens when our perception of some aspect of reality is exposed to be false. We discover that what we thought was real was only an illusion. Typically, when we become disillusioned, we experience mental, emotional, even spiritual anguish.

When things are going well in our lives, we might agree, in principle, that someone who exposes our false perceptions of reality has done us a service. But when it actually happens to us, it is a different story. Why? Because, as we go about living our lives, we put our hope and confidence in our firm convictions and perceptions of what is real. We act on them. We take joy in them. When these convictions and perceptions are exposed as illusions, our eyes are opened and the truth is revealed. Consequently, we are left with a perception of reality that was not what we had expected or had come to believe was true. We become *dis*-illusioned.

Stages of Disillusionment

The stages of disillusionment are not dissimilar to the stages of grief (denial, anger, bargaining, depression, acceptance). In the face of disillusionment, we tend to defend our illusions and reject any presumption of reality that undoes our idealistic view of things (denial).

Next, we may become embarrassed because we were caught believing in something now proven false. We feel foolish. For a while, the embarrassment may feed our denial. But eventually, embarrassment gives way to anger, discouragement, and resentment (or some combination of the three).

Finally, we have three choices: 1) reattach to the illusion, which is to live in denial, 2) exist in a state of disillusioned paralysis, or 3) embrace the new reality.

Disillusioned with God

Unmet expectations are not usually met with positive reactions. We tie our hopes to what we expect and when those expectations are not realized, our hopes are dashed! Then we become disillusioned with the person or institution we trusted; the picture we thought we had of reality turned out to be an illusion.

Sometimes people break promises and when they do it hurts. But sometimes we misread situations and develop false or unrealistic expectations of others. It is important that we have right expectations of God. Many have developed wrong expectations of God because they never learned about Him, His ways, or His promises, or they were given wrong information. They have projected *their* logic and reasoning onto *Him* and have based their expectations on a faulty understanding of His nature, heart, and purposes. Consequently, when God does not do what they expect, they lose heart, become discouraged or even disillusioned. We must be careful not to define God based on the faulty human examples we have observed.

The Questions

With these insights in mind, let's consider the three questions mentioned above. The first two are as follows. Our answer to the third will hinge upon our consideration of the first two.

1) Can God be trusted?

This first question addresses our need to know who God is and to understand His nature? The answers to this question will reveal God's trustworthiness.

2) What can God be trusted to do?

This question addresses the issue of God's purposes and promises. The answer to this question will reveal the practical ways He wants to be involved in our lives, the promises He has made, and His purpose for our lives.

Answers

The first question can be reworded *Does He care?* In one of my favorite passages of Scripture, Moses is recounting for Israel the awe-filled day when God descended upon Mt. Sinai (Deuteronomy 5; Exodus 19-20). The people had been consecrated and were gathered at the foot of the mountain. They were not to touch the mountain, nor were they to break through in order to see the Presence of the Lord. But they *were* allowed to hear God speaking to Moses as He gave him what we call the Ten Commandments. They "trembled with fear" when they "saw the thunder and lightning and heard the trumpet and saw the mountain in smoke (Exodus 20:18)." They stayed back and told Moses, "Speak to us yourself and we will listen. But do not have God speak to us or we will die." God was listening. Moses told the people forty years later:

> The LORD heard you when you spoke to me and the LORD said to me, "I have heard what this people said to you. Everything they said was good. Oh, that their hearts would be inclined to fear me and keep all my commands always, so *that it might go well with them and their children forever* (Deuteronomy 5:28-29)!"

Can you hear the heart of God in that verse? I always have. I can hear God longing for the hearts of the people and longing for their wellbeing and for the wellbeing of their children!

The disciples encountered a storm that threatened their lives. One evening they were in a boat headed to the other side of the Sea of Galilee when a "furious squall came up" (Mark 4:37). Waves nearly swamped the boat. Fearing for their lives they came to Jesus who was asleep in the back of the boat (another divine absurdity?). They woke Jesus up and cried out, "Teacher, don't you care if we drown?" You know the rest of the story. He calmed the threatening storm. Jesus *did* care whether they drowned or not. God cares.

The second question is about God's purpose for our lives and can be reworded *What has He promised to do for me?*

Perhaps you have heard of the so-called *prosperity gospel?* One of the objections I have with that particular slant on the gospel is that, even when its teachers and adherents try to address a topic unrelated to personal material blessing, they invariably arrive again at the discussion of how we can be abundantly blessed.

There is no denying that the blessings afforded to us as God's children are abundant. But those blessings are not the chief purpose of the Christian life. You can see that purpose in Mary, the sister of Martha and Lazarus, sitting at the feet of Jesus, attending to Him

113

(Luke 10:38-42). That's our purpose: attending to Him, being available to Him, concerning ourselves with that which blesses Him! This is a major sea change from what we were before we became Christians. It is no longer about us! It is about Him and His purposes. It is about our transformation from being self-absorbed to being self-less. You can see how important such a posture is to waiting on the Lord. When we begin to see the big picture it puts our personal needs in perspective.

In the following passage, we again see and hear the heart of God, this time addressing His own purpose for and involvement in our lives.

> "For I know the plans I have for you," declares the LORD, *"plans to prosper you and not to harm you, plans to give you hope and a future.* Then you will call upon me and come and pray to me, and I will listen to you. You will seek me and find me when you seek me with all your heart. I will be found by you," declares the LORD (Jeremiah 29:11-14a, emphasis mine).

Anyone with a good grasp of the Bible's message in its entirety recognizes that this is and always has been the heart of God. God always has a plan and is always open to those who come to Him surrendering their hearts in humility.

Of course, this discussion has not exhausted the Scriptures that could be referenced in support of God's care and God's promises to us; His interest in us. But we already knew these things, didn't we? In fact the issue isn't really whether He cares, has made promises, or has proven His desire to be involved in our lives. The major issue is revealed in the third big question.

3) Do we trust Him?

Can God be trusted to do what is best for us? Is He attentive to us? Does He care? We can see from the discussion above that God is intentional, positive, available, and that He values sincerity. He wants to bless us, encourage us, partner with us, hear from us, respond to us, and give guidance to us. He is not just expectantly watching over us but also over our children and their children and beyond! Psalm 147:11 tells us something of the response God wants from us when it says, "The LORD delights in those who fear him, who put their hope in his unfailing love."

In light of these things, we have a decision to make. *If* we have discovered that His heart *is* inclined toward us, that His promises are real, and if we have believed the overwhelming preponderance of evidence that points to God's faithfulness, are we, in fact, ready to align ourselves with His purpose, and place our lives in His hands? Once we read about God in the Bible, and begin to discover who He is and what He has promised, we realize that God can be trusted. He meets and exceeds our expectations! But the question still remains: *Do we trust Him?* Are we willing to leave off all of our efforts to control our circumstances and outcomes and allow God to work in our lives? How do we navigate through all of the experiences and voices that tell us not to trust anyone, let alone a God we cannot see? It is at this point that we must realize that an entire arsenal of strength has been made available to us, accessible day by day as we engage in the very strong act of waiting on the Lord.

Before moving forward...

In this chapter I have not tried to give a full exposition of all that Scripture reveals concerning God's heart and His promises. The reader likely knows a good deal about these things. The salient point has been that, if we have a genuine biblical Christian worldview, if we have accepted the word of God as an authentic record of God's divine self-revelation, and if we have made the commitment to allow God and His Word to be the final authority for our lives, then we must ultimately agree that the Bible does paint a picture of a loving God who can be trusted and who has promised to care for us. This leaves us with only one big question: *Do we trust Him?* Answering this question is and, then again, is not a binary decision. It *is* in the sense that we either trust Him or we don't. And yet sometimes we find ourselves in the same position as the concerned father of Mark 9 who said, "Lord, I believe. Help thou my unbelief!" If this describes you, don't wait any longer! Cry out to God and ask Him to help you trust Him fully!

11

Waiting Principles

We have seen in previous chapters how God wants to partner with us as He carries out His kingdom purposes. Hopefully, through the various examples of lives lived in the middle (chapters 1, 4-7), the detailed stages of God's process (chapter 2), the "curtain" passages and God's participation (chapter 3), and all that has been said thus far about waiting on the Lord (chapters 8-10), you are beginning to see how it all fits together. In chapter 13 I will help with that.

In this chapter, I want to share four insights, leaving a fifth for the next chapter, that will help breathe value *and hope* into your times of waiting (helping you make sense of what *is* and *is not* happening), give you insight into the inner workings of the spiritual realm, help you tap into your God-given authority, and realign your focus and your priorities toward God.

Factoring in the Spiritual Realm

We are caught up in an epic cosmic conflict. Just as God inhabits eternity His domain is the spiritual realm. He is *spirit* (John 4:24).[26] This is not to say that he does not operate in human time and history. Rather, our existence is surrounded by and permeated with the spiritual realm and is, in fact, driven by spiritual forces that we cannot see. In the spiritual realm there are evil spiritual entities who wish God ill and who want to harm God's creation, and more importantly, God's *chief* creation: humanity. In the spiritual realm, things hang in the balance that we could not possibly fathom. The forces of good and evil collide and the collision comes to bear upon us as we wait on the Lord.

In chapter 3 we considered Daniel's delayed answer from God. Daniel was fasting because he was desperate to hear from God (Daniel 10:2-3). Then, an archangel appeared to him saying,[27]

> Do not be afraid, Daniel. Since the first day that you set your mind to gain un-

120

derstanding and to humble yourself before your God, your words were heard,
and I have come in response to them.
But the prince of the Persian kingdom
resisted me twenty-one days. Then Michael, one of the chief princes, came to
help me, because I was detained there
with the king of Persia (Daniel 10:12-
13).

Consider the ramifications of this "curtain"
passage upon your own prayer times and sea-
sons of waiting on the Lord! Does it help you
to realize that battles are waged in heaven
over your prayers? This passage speaks to the
value of our prayers, our intentional waiting
upon the Lord, and it certainly gives us insight into workings of the spiritual realm. But
it also says something about the importance
of God's timing.

God's Timing

Because God sees the end from the beginning (Ecclesiastes 3:11, Isaiah 43:13, 2 Timo-
thy 1:9, Hebrews 4:3, 1 Peter 1:20, Revelation
17:8), promises to work all things for good to
those who love Him and are committed to
Him (Romans 8:28, Philippians 1:6), and has
granted free will to His human creation

(Proverbs 16:9, Joshua 24:15, Deuteronomy 30:19-20, Genesis 2:16-17, etc.), we must recognize that timing is an important factor. We cannot know what is coming nor can we see what God sees unless He allows us to. Therefore, because of His heart and character, because of the eternal nature of God's plan and existence, and because we live out our lives in the midst of a cosmic conflict, we must trust God to work on our behalf according to His timing. But not only do we trust Him to work on our behalf, we also hear the call to work *with* God as He fulfills His will in time and history.[28]

You can see how an understanding of God's timing might bring encouragement to you when you have been waiting on the Lord for something you urgently desire. God alone knows how to work all things together and knows just when to open doors and when to close them. He alone knows what He is keeping you *from* (see Genesis 20:6)!

Reckoning unto God

While the word *reckoning* has several shades of meaning in English, in the New Testament (*logizomai*) it generally means "to credit, to consider." Of the forty times the word is used in the New Testament, seventeen of those occurrences are what we could call "vertical." That is, in those verses the word describes an aspect of "reckoning" or "accounting" in divine-human relationships. Of those seventeen times, it is used almost exclusively in terms of *God* doing the reckoning. For example, the Bible tells us that Abraham believed God and it was reckoned or accounted to him as righteousness (Gen 15:6, Romans 4:3). But in Hebrews 11:19, we see that Abraham did some reckoning as well.

In Chapter 1, we briefly considered Abraham's willingness to sacrifice Isaac (p. 16). In reference to that event, Hebrews 11:19 says,

> Abraham reasoned [reckoned/logizomai] that God could raise the dead, and figuratively speaking, he did receive Isaac back from death.

Since Abraham had believed God's promise that Isaac would be born, and since he had received that promise (Isaac was with him), he knew that God would follow through with His promise to bless all nations through Isaac (Genesis 12:2-3), and that his offspring through Isaac would be so numerous as to be impossible to count (Genesis 15:4-5). When God called upon him to sacrifice Isaac (Genesis 22), Abraham *reckoned* (logizomai) that, if necessary, God would raise Isaac from the dead in order to keep His promises!

So, reckoning is a *faith calculation*. It is not vain hope that something good might happen, positive thinking in a desperate moment, or wishful thinking, but rather an accounting based on the promises of God. The principle of reckoning says that, while it may seem that the details of our lives are in the hands of employers, politicians, court systems, or even in our own hands, on the contrary, it is God who is in control of every detail of our lives. However, to enjoy the benefits of reckoning we must participate with God! How? By releasing God to do what only He can do! This means that instead of trying to force or manipulate others into blessing us, we declare our trust in the Lord, inviting Him to take full control of every aspect of our lives. We reckon the details of our lives unto God and, by faith, receive all the promises of God! This is not wishful thinking because our reckoning is based on what we know God has promised to do! In reckoning we declare what God has already promised.

God is Our Portion

Finally, a curious yet powerful truth can be seen in the inheritances that were meted out to the twelve tribes of Israel once they had taken hold in the promised land of Canaan.

In Numbers 18:20,[29] the LORD said to Aaron, "You shall have no inheritance in their land nor own any portion among them; *I am your portion and your inheritance among the sons of Israel* (emphasis mine)." While all the other tribes received plots of land that would be their perpetual possession, the Levites did not. Instead, they inherited the Lord!

Long before the Levites, God said something similar to Abraham. Sometime after defeating the kings that kidnapped his nephew Lot (Genesis 14), and after having refused to accept any of the plunder from the hands of the King of Sodom, we gather that Abraham is afraid and perhaps feeling that he may have missed a chance to prosper. In Genesis 15:1, we read,

> After this, the word of the Lord came to Abram in a vision: "Do not be afraid, Abram. I am your shield, your very great reward."

In essence, God said Abraham, "Don't worry! At the end of the day you get Me!"

If we are honest with ourselves, there are times when what we want is the stuff! When we are walking in the flesh, the idea of God as our reward instead of the stuff we want is not appealing. But spiritual maturity calls us to deeper places than that. Understanding God as our portion realigns our priorities and directs our gaze to that which is most important: God! Ultimately, we begin to value the privilege of partnering with God more than the things we hope to receive from God. We begin to realize that, like the Levites of old, our inheritance is not earthly, temporal gain, but God Himself. He is our portion!

A profound example of both the concept of God as our portion and of the power of waiting on the Lord can be found in Lamentations 3:19-26. In the midst of the horror of utter tragedy, Jeremiah wrote:

> Remember my affliction and my wandering, the wormwood and bitterness. Surely my soul remembers and is bowed down within me. This I recall to my mind, therefore I have hope. The LORD'S loving kindnesses indeed never cease, for His compassions never fail. [They] are new every morning; great is your faithfulness. "*The LORD is my portion*," says my soul, "Therefore I have hope in Him." The LORD is good to *those who wait for Him*, to the person who seeks Him. *It is* good that he

waits silently for the salvation of the LORD (emphasis mine).

The deeper we go into God the more we realize that nothing could be a greater reward than God Himself!

Before moving forward...

So, how do we begin to wait on the Lord? Well, there is no replacement for simply doing it. But what does that look like? How does it begin? We must first recognize and acknowledge the ways in which we attempt to exert control over our own circumstances, turning those areas over to God. Then we must intentionally begin to wait on the Lord which means we refrain from trying to force things to go our way. We begin to replace worry with faith and trust. This does not mean that we *never* act but it does mean that we act according to God's will and not our own.

In *Indiana Jones and the Last Crusade*, Indiana must take a "leap of faith" in order to proceed to the Holy Grail. Standing at the edge of a huge chasm, he takes a step onto what looks like thin air in hopes that, somehow, his feet will land on solid ground, which of course they do. Waiting on the Lord can

127

seem like that. When it seems like we should be taking the safe route and finding a way to "make our own luck" in some situation we really care about, it is counterintuitive to do nothing, as it were, in hopes that God will take over. But as we have already seen, waiting on the Lord is not doing nothing!

Before we are done, there is one more important insight I need to share!

12

Purpose

There is no way to overestimate the power of purpose. In this chapter, I would like to walk with you through some important realities, if you will, that say something profound about human purpose. I admit up front that this chapter will perhaps be a bit more theological than the others, but the treasure gleaned at the end will be worth the reader's struggle, should there be one.

What does God know?

Would you agree that God knows everything? That's one of the prerequisites for being God, right? Not only that, but because of God's omniscience, we can also say that it is impossible for God to have a new thought. We can't surprise God or "spring" something on God. Would you also agree that God is eternal and has existed eternally in three persons: Father, Son, and Holy Spirit? This is basic Christian belief.

It is estimated that 107 billion humans have ever existed.[30] Regardless of whether we would agree with that number, based on our religious views of Creation, everyone would agree that the number of humans who have ever existed must be a finite number. For Christians, who believe in an end to history as we know it, we agree that, when all is said and done, it will be a finite number of humans who will *ever* exist.

So, God who has existed eternally and who knows all that is, ever has been, or ever will be knowable, has always known that He would create humanity, and that that number of humans would be finite. Further, He knew that *you* would be one of those creations. From these truths I can assert that you have always been in God's heart! He has always known about you!

This does not mean that you are eternally existing (though you *will* live forever), or that in some way you have divine substance, etc. Nor does it mean that you had some pre-incarnate existence before being born on this earth. What it means is that our intentional God has always had a plan that included you! This truth is at the heart of your purpose on this earth.

The Eternal Fellowship of the Godhead

We also know that in God's eternal Trinitarian existence, the three divine Persons have existed in an eternal divine fellowship with one another. Jesus prayed, "And now, Father, glorify me in your presence with the glory I had with you before the world began (John 17:5)." In that same prayer He prayed, "Father, I want those you have given me to be with me where I am, and to see my glory, the glory you have given me because you loved me before the creation of the world (v. 24)."

We also know that God is love (1 John 4:8). Because the Godhead has dwelled eternally in a love relationship with one another, and because God *is* love, we can also say that, not only has God always known that you would exist, but you exist because of His love! Love is why God created us. Not because He was incomplete. God is Self-sufficient and does not need us. In one place, God said, "If I were hungry I would not tell you, for the world is mine, and all that is in it (Psalm 50:12)." He did not create us because He was

131

running short on self-confidence or because He was lacking in completeness. God is complete in Himself. But God is *love*! His desire is that the great Triune fellowship of the Godhead would overflow into His creation. He invites us into that eternal relationship that we might experience His love, not because of His need, but because He is good!

Matt Chandler, author of *The Explicit Gospel*, dismisses this idea because he cannot imagine that it is God's priority to fellowship with His creation. He refers to God's "glorious self-regard."[31]

> Most of us have been told that God created the universe, created all that exists within the universe, and employed the depth of his omnipotence and omniscience to create this because he desired to fellowship with man. Have you heard this line of thinking before? It's a very sweet idea, and it would be a great slogan for a Christian motivational poster if it weren't for what the Bible *actually teaches*, which is that this idea is almost blasphemous. Are we to believe that God—in his infinite perfection—was lonely?[32]

The author continues on with proof that, at

least in this area, he has misunderstood the heart of God.

Sometimes, an idea that we consider to be an extreme error causes us to settle upon error in order to combat it. The fact that God was not lonely and didn't *need* to create humanity in order to be complete in Himself does not require that we render Him incapable of creating humanity as a result of His love. This thinking is too steeped in Calvinism to recognize that God is capable of being complete in Himself *and* of creating the human race so that we could know Him in His greatness and enjoy His fellowship! Chandler would have us believe that, because God is so focused on His own glory, He is driven to restore fallen humanity in order to correct all the broken images of Himself. He depicts a narcissistic God who only helps us so that He can help Himself. Not only are thoughts like these fallacious, but they don't address the question of why God created us in the first place.

Has God's plan failed?

There is one more thing to consider before we are finished with the concept of *purpose*. For many years, I wrestled with a question that I was afraid to ask out loud. The question had to do with hell. My struggle went something like this: when all of history as we know it comes to an end, and we finally reach the furthest point in time that the Bible envisions—the Second Coming (Matthew 24:29-31), the White Throne judgment (Revelation 20:11), and all that is described in the last two chapters of Revelation, etc.—won't we have to admit that, if people go to hell, there has been eternal loss, regardless of how many go to heaven? Has God's "experiment" failed? In order to address this question, we will have a take a look at the "Plan B" mentality so common in Christian thinking.

"Plan B" Mentality

The "Plan B" mentality goes like this: God's first plan was that Adam and Eve would be perfect and live harmoniously in the Garden of Eden forever. Because they sinned against God and caused the fall of mankind, God had to go to Plan B. The incarnation, life, death, burial, and resurrection of Jesus Christ, and even His being slain before the foundation of the world (Revelation 13:8), all became necessary when God's original plan was thwarted after Adam and Eve succumbed to temptation. God was forced to come and die for us in order to salvage His broken plan.

Such a view has God being caught by surprise and operating in problem-solving mode. If all that has been said above about God's eternal nature and omniscience is true, then we cannot subscribe to a Plan B mentality.

So, then what *can* be said about God's ultimate intention in this epic He has invited us into? Could we say that within God's nature is sacrificial love? What is the message of the gospel if not "I am unsurpassably, unreachably holy, I am love, I am unselfish, I will love, I will sacrifice so that those I love may be made able to love also." If the message in the end is Jesus, then that must have been the message in the beginning, indeed, from eternity! So, far from the shock we imagine God must have felt as His creation fell, we must instead admit that the fall of humanity was an inevitable step on the path toward a universal realization by all creation that God is Holy and there is none beside Him; that God is love and there is nothing He won't do to reach us (barring a violation of His own nature and character) even unto death! Can we view the entirety of salvation history as God's way of introducing Himself to us? Could it be that from eternity God's plan was to invite His special creation into fellowship with Himself and that the only way that that fellowship could be lasting would be for creation to take an epic journey in which it would discover who God is and how it could enter into fellowship with Him? Can we allow that this was God's way of saying, "I want you to know that I am Holy, I am Love, and I am willing to die in order to fellowship with you because I created you! I am Trinitarian in my nature and have invited you into that Trinitarian fellowship, and the best way for you to reach Me as Father is through My Son, Jesus Christ, and through the agency of My Holy Spirit"?

Profound Recklessness

Imagine the profound recklessness of a God who is willing to create, not pre-programmed robots who were predestined to sin, but free-will beings with the capacity to experience the depths of His love or the depths of hell. Beings with the capacity to worship, murder, idolize. Then try and fathom that He did this all for the sake of displaying His holiness, sharing the unsearchable riches of His love, compassion, joy, and the opportunity to share pure relational connection with the objects of His love! Talk about divine imagination! At the heart of this picture is a God who is holy and wants to share that holiness; a God who is love and wants to share that love.

Foreknowledge?

But what is to be said about God's fore-knowledge that, even though it was not pre-destined to be so, some *would* murder and ultimately choose not to be with Him? What is to be said about God's willingness to bring beings into existence that would live forever, knowing that some of those beings would, in the end, experience eternal punishment and separation? How precious and awesome must be the fellowship that God has in store for those who freely worship Him that He would risk such pain? We must allow that God, who is love, knew that many of his human crea-tions would choose not to fellowship with Him. It is foolish to think, as some do, that this somehow brings Him glory. On the con-trary, if God is love, the eternal loss of any of His human creations has to bring Him pain. And yet, He *did* create with this reality in mind. What does this say about the surpas-sing value God has placed on those of His cre-ation that *do* want to fellowship with Him? What does this profound truth say about our purpose?

Before moving forward...

Your reaction to these things should be

amazement that Almighty God, who does not *need* you, *wants* you! What does this say about your purpose on this earth? Your reaction should be to stand in awe that the God of the universe (a title woefully inadequate) knows your name and cares about you!

13

Afterword

One of my favorite entries in the classic devotional *Streams in the Desert*, comes on August 16.[33] Interestingly enough, the entry is about waiting. But what grabbed my attention one day while reading it was the phrase "to 'brighten the corner' where we are." With my imagination stoked, I began to imagine a man caught up in a dream or a vision where he found himself walking along some country or city road, when all of a sudden he would be "inserted" into the real life situation of some obscure person from the past—some unknown, unheralded person who "brightened the corner" where they lived and died. A person who, regardless of his or her circumstances and relative obscurity, would have been found (had they been noticed at all) living in such a way as to be found faithful; persevering; standing in the gap; or as Frank Laubach has it, "making each hour gloriously rich."[34] People who were faithfully filling their posts, fulfilling their duties before God, travailing in prayer...people of God, but common in the eyes of humanity.

That's life in the middle. Right now. Today. Right where you are. Having believed in the promise but not yet having enjoyed its complete fulfillment. Participating with God everywhere you hear His call to do so. Longing for the vision to come to pass—wrestling with God if need be—and ready to let *your* vision die so that *His* vision for you can live.

Life in the middle is not slowed down by delays, postponements, and cancellations. On the contrary, it sees these as opportunities to wait on the Lord, knowing that "Faithful *is* he that calleth you, who also will do *it* (1 Thessalonians 5:24, KJV)."

There's no time like the present to begin living faithfully in the middle. It begins in the secret place—in the prayer closet—where we have the promise that our Father, "who sees what is done in secret," will reward us. It occurs to me that, while we may feel that we are living in obscurity, none of God's children goes unnoticed to Him. And when we remember that our greatest reward is God Himself, then joy begins to flow as we live life in the middle.

Life in the Middle

Discovery Guide

The purpose of this *Discovery Guide* is to help the reader dig further into Scripture and the book *Life in the Middle* in order to solidify his or her grasp of the concepts shared within.

God's Process

Bartimaeus

1. Read Mark 10:46-52 and review chapter 2 (especially the first four paragraphs) and chapter 5 of *Life in the Middle*.

2. What did Bartimaeus believe about Jesus (read verses 47-48, 51-52)?

3. How did Bartimaeus know anything about Jesus?

4. Though Bartimaeus was blind, he had a vision. What was it?

5. Search the Gospel of Mark for any event, prior to this one with Bartimaeus, that would have indicated to him, had he heard about it, that Jesus could heal him of his blindness.

6. What was Bartimaeus's *divine imagination*?

7. How much time passed between the moment in Bartimaeus's life when he realized that Jesus could heal him and the moment when he had the opportunity to cry out to Jesus?

8. Is there a "Peninnah" in this story?

9. When Jesus healed Bartimaeus, what did he do in response?

10. If Jesus stopped by your house today and asked, "What do you want me to do for you?" what would you ask for?

Participation with God

Jehoshaphat

1. Read 2 Chronicles 20:1-25 and review chapters 1, 2, 8-9, and 11 of *Life in the Middle.*

2. What was happening "in the natural" (read verses 1-4)?

3. What was Jehoshaphat's response to the threat?

4. Read verses 5-12 and put into words Jehoshaphat's worldview. What did he believe about God?

5. In what way did Jehoshaphat "reckon" unto God? How did God's promises and past actions impact Jehoshaphat's expectation for the immediate future?

6. What spiritual "weapons" did Jehoshaphat enlist in this situation (see verses 3, 18-22)?

7. Although this event with Jehoshaphat and Judah happened in a relatively short period of time, do you see any of the elements of God's process in this story?

8. What would Jehoshaphat and Judah have done "in the natural" had they not consulted and waited on God? What natural instincts and control mechanisms did they have to put aside in order to relinquish control to God?

The "Curtain" Passages

Cornelius (Acts 10)

1. Read Acts 10 (focusing on verses 1-6, 24-33, 44-48), and review chapters 2, 3, the discussion on God's timing in chapter 11 of *Life in the Middle*.

2. What makes this a "Curtain" passage (read verse 4)?

3. What happened in heaven that "triggered" Cornelius's vision and visit from the angel?

4. In what way did God invite Cornelius to participate with Him (read verse 5)?

5. What was God trying to bring about for Cornelius, his relatives, and close friends (read verses 24, 44-48)?

6. Read Psalm 56:8, Revelation 5:8, Revelation 8:3-4 and discover how these passages connect as "curtain" passages with Acts 10.

7. If God "saves up prayers" for a certain time, what does this suggest concerning the importance of God's timing?

Waiting on the Lord

Lamentations

1. Read the book of Lamentations (particularly 3:19-26) and chapters 8 and 11 of *Life in the Middle*.

2. What was the writer of Lamentations (whom most agree was Jeremiah) waiting for (start with 3:19-26)?

3. What did the author remember that pulled him back from the brink of despair (verses 21-23)?

4. What are the implications of the word *therefore* in verse 24? What is the writer saying?

5. As you read through the short book of Lamentations, make a list of all that has been lost. Then, consider the significance of verses 24-25. Compare the value of having God as your portion in the face of such loss.

6. In what way could God be the portion of a woman who had to consume her child (2:20)?

7. In what way might it comfort you to know that God is your portion? How could that truth be made real in your situations?

APPENDIX

Dynamic Concepts

It is important to recognize that the concepts shared in *Life in the Middle* are dynamic. That is, they are not "cut and dried" concepts that can be found the same way in every Bible story. Instead, what we find are shades of these concepts that work themselves out in varying ways in different Bible situations. The same will be found to be true in our lives as well.

The phrase used in this book "between promise and fulfillment" might throw some people off. I considered using the word *hope* instead but I didn't feel it was completely true to what we see in Scripture. Sometimes the "promise" is our *perception* of what God has promised (thus our discussion of *disillusionment* in chapter 10). For example, the pain

Hannah experienced as she lived faithfully in the middle was lived between what she felt strongly had been promised to her based on her gender. As a woman she had every reason to expect that she would bear children. As a godly woman she had even more reason to think that, as part of God's blessings, she would bear children. So, we can see that Hannah had a sense of a promise that she would have children. It was the strength of this expectation that made her pain so unbearable. In the end, we discover that she was not wrong, she just had to adjust to God's plan.

The story did not end with Hannah's pregnancy. She had to wait nine months for the child to be born. She had no way of knowing it would be a boy (as per her request in 1 Samuel 1:11). Her faith and the reality of her pregnancy told her that God was involved and that indeed she would have a boy that could then be dedicated to God and given to Eli to live with him in the temple, but time would tell if she was right. This is supported by Elkanah's statement in verse 23, "Do what seems best to you. Remain until you have weaned him; only may the LORD confirm His word." In verses 24-28 we see that this is when Hannah reminds Eli who she is and of her intentions. Would Eli accept this? Would all of this happen just as she envisioned?

Habakkuk's story is similar in that he too was operating with a righteous expectation (God's correction of the wicked in Judah, Habakkuk 1:1-4). This expectation was so strong that it created frustration in Habakkuk the longer it went unrealized. His sense of God's promise was on point: God would indeed correct the wicked, but He would do it in a way that would launch Habakkuk into even deeper dissatisfaction. When he finally realized that tremendous vision was attached to what God was doing, Habakkuk began a fresh new phase of living in the middle. Now, he has been promised that "The earth will be filled with the knowledge of the glory of the Lord, as the waters cover the sea (2:14)" and yet his death would come before he would see that day arrive. His faith would have to suffice (2:4).

In the case of Joseph (Genesis 37-47), he had no way of knowing where God was taking him. The only sense of promise he had was his dreams in which his family was submissive to him. So, Joseph endured the next twenty-three years with no idea where he was headed and certainly with a sense of the unfairness of having been robbed of a future by his brothers. We could say that only in looking back over all that God had done in his life would Joseph have been able to recognize that he

was living faithfully between promise and fulfillment.

NOTES

Chapter 2 God's Process

[1] This could be indicated as the *spiritual* status quo. However, sometimes our desire for certain things may at first appear to be typical "horizontal" pursuits. In Hannah's story (see *Part 2*), her desire was for a child—surely a natural desire. But she discovers that her desire for a son intersects with *God's* desire for her to have a son that she would be willing to dedicate to a life of spiritual service. So, it is spiritual vision we are interested in but our entrance may at first seem non-spiritual. It could be said that God works in our desires to redirect our gaze toward what He wants to do. Moses wanted to personally defend his Hebrew brothers. God wanted to bring about the deliverance of every Hebrew, something Moses could not have done on his own.

[2] A great question which can help to clarify what a person's real passion is: "If there were no obstacles or barriers, what would you do for the kingdom of God?"

NOTES

3 I am aware that there are various ways people have construed the concept of the death of the vision, none of which I am particularly familiar with. What I share in this book is the view I have arrived at from my study of Scripture over the past twenty-two years.

4 This is the basis on which Paul can declare in Romans 5:1-5 that we rejoice in tribulation, and again in Philippians 4:4, "rejoice always and again I say rejoice."

5 Hannah Whitall Smith, *The Christian's Secret of a Happy Life*, (New York: Fleming H. Revell Company, 1916), 34.

Chapter 3 Participating With God

6 Spiritual warfare is not first and foremost about obtaining earthly goals, etc., but it very often is about fighting a spiritual battle so that victory can be experienced in the natural.

7 On the grounds that we know that Elisha in himself did not have the authority to grant the king a victory, and since Elisha was an authentic prophet, and since we do not see God rejecting or correcting Elisha in this situation, we can infer that God had in some way communicated with the prophet that a victory had been granted—grounded inference.

8 Some believe that Daniel 10 I an account of an encounter with the pre-incarnate Christ in a theophanic appearance. However, as the passage continues, we read that this "being" was "detained" by the Prince of Persia (understood to be the evil spiritual prince over the territory of Persia). Since the Second Person of the godhead cannot be detained by an evil force, this being cannot be the pre-incarnate Christ.

I assume this to be an archangel (the word archangel/archangelos is only found twice in the New Testament and not at all in the OT.) Was it Gabriel? We must first consider whether Gabriel was an archangel at all. The NT only names one archangel, Michael (Jude 9). That said, tradition has elevated Gabriel to this level, though the Bible never refers to him as such. Nevertheless, the being that Daniel encounters is obviously quite powerful and seems to have an affect greater than perhaps a "regular" angel would have. So, assuming that this is an archangel and accounting for the fact that Michael comes to help, I believe we probably have two archangels here. However, Gabriel had just made an appearance to Daniel in the previous chapter and Daniel does not have the same response in that situation did in Dan. 10. This strengthens the claim that the being in Dan. 10 is the pre-incarnate Christ in a theophanic appearance. I am still unable to accept, however, that the pre-incarnate Christ would need the help of Michael to press through an answer to Daniel.

At any rate, nothing is lost or gained from the message by assuming or not assuming that the unnamed being in Dan. 10 is an archangel, but identifying the being as the pre-incarnate Christ would be inconsistent with what we know about the theophanic appearances, the pre-incarnate Christ, and the Second Person of the godhead.

9 Joseph Ratzinger, *Jesus of Nazareth*, (San Francisco: Ignatius Press, 2007), 57.

Chapter 4 Hannah

10 I have gleaned some background information on the sociological effects of barrenness in ancient times from Jeremy Schipper and Candida Moss, *Disability Studies*

and Biblical Literature, Palgrave McMillan, 2011), 13-27.

Chapter 5   Hannah and Peninnah

[11] According to 1 Samuel 1:5, Peninnah had "sons and daughters." By my calculations, that is at least four children.

[12] *The Glass Menagerie.*

[13] Dallas Willard's translation of Galatians 6:2, normally translated "Carry each other's burdens."

Chapter 6   Elkanah's Offer

[14] A. W. Tozer, *The Attributes of God, Volume 1*, (Camphill, PA: Wing Spread Publishers, 1997), 154.

[15] Frances Hamerstrom, *An Eagle to the Sky,* (Lions Press, 1988).

[16] Bald Eagle-Nesting and Young, quoting Hamerstrom @ http://www.baldeagleinfo.com/eagle /eagle4.html

Chapter 8   Waiting on the Lord

[17] No matter how much we preach and teach that our trials develop character, etc. (Romans 5:1-5; James 1:2-4), we still show up every week at church praying for God to deliver us instantly from all of our troubles! But who among us is asking for extra troubles just so that we can develop more character?

[18] Parrott, *Control Freak*, page 2-3.

NOTES

[19] It should somewhere be mentioned that the kind of waiting depicted in the Bible is that which is done with experience under the belt. That is, the one waiting has learned that the One being waited on is faithful!

[20] Willem A. VanGeneren, Gen. Ed., The New International Dictionary of Old Testament Theology & Exegesis, Volume 3, (Grand Rapids, MI: Zondervan, 1997), 892-894.

[21] Warren Baker, Eugene Carpenter, The Complete Word Study Dictionary: Old Testament, (Chattanooga, TN: AMG Publishers, 2003), 986.

[22] Dallas Willard, *The Spirit of the Disciplines*, 153, 158.

[23] Richard Foster, *Celebration of Discipline*, (New York: Harper & Row, 1978), 96.

[24] Ibid.

Chapter 10   Three Big Questions

[25] Trust is "dependence on something future or contingent" (Webster online)

Chapter 11   Waiting Principles

[26] Using a small 's' here does not negate that the Holy Spirit is God. John's point is to emphasis the word spirit over flesh; since God is spirit He must be worshipped in spirit and in truth. I have no real qualms with the word here being capitalized but the structure in the Greek is attributive and to some degree making the word spirit emphatic.

NOTES

[27] See note 8 above.

[28] Evidence of the importance of God's timing: God saving up our prayers (collecting tears, Cornelius, Revelation), Daniel's answer being delayed, David being directed to wait until he heard the "sound of a going," etc.

[29] See also Deuteronomy 10:9, 12:12, 14:27-29; Joshua 13:33, Ezekiel 44:28.

Chapter 12   Purpose

[30] (http://www.bbc.com/news/magazine-16870579)

[31]Matt Chandler (with Jared Wilson), *The Explicit Gospel*, (Wheaton, ILL: Crossway, 2012), 32.

[32] Ibid.

Chapter 13   Afterword

[33] L. B. Cowman, *Streams in the Desert*, ed. Jim Reimann, (Grand Rapids, MI: Zondervan Publishing, 1997), 313.

[34] In Richard Foster's, *Prayer*, (New York: Harper Collins, 1992), 125.